Masculinity and Femininity

Masculinity and Femininity

Designs in Sexual Intimacies

T. HOOGSTEEN

RESOURCE *Publications* · Eugene, Oregon

MASCULINITY AND FEMININITY
Designs in Sexual Intimacies

Resource Publications
An Imprint of Wipf and Stock Publishers
199 W. 8th Ave., Suite 3
Eugene, OR 97401

www.wipfandstock.com

PAPERBACK ISBN: 979-8-3852-6485-8
HARDCOVER ISBN: 979-8-3852-6486-5
EBOOK ISBN: 979-8-3852-6487-2

VERSION NUMBER 11/26/25

Rev. Dr. William T. Koopmans

For pastoring

Contents

Preface

FACT ONE. SPIRITS OF the age frame the designs in human sexuality. Free-for-all voices assert eagerness to break down biblical barriers, advertise satisfactions of, and demand social acceptance for abortion, contraception, premarital sex, prostitution, pederasty, divorce, pedophilia, homosexuality, adultery, polygamy/polyamory, same-sex unions, reproductive freedoms, and childless marriages. All sorts of now conventional sexualities run the gamut of perversion.

Fact Two. Men shape and dictate the spirits of the age. In paganizing worlds, then, men dominate women. Given this dominance, in civilizing environments, men may find equality with women an interesting ideal and women may see complementarity with men a fascinating model. Yet, women remain the secondary gender, men inventing necessary gods to revalidate this long antiquated social order.

Fact Three. In the twentieth century, post-World War Two, to maintain male dominance, hyper-masculinity or masochism, despite amplifying feminist voices, men ruled the gender revolutions—for male satisfaction. Since, throughout this world, whatever the fighting spirits in feminism, not much happens without approval of and benefit for men. Therefore, to control the social revolting on the gender barriers, Western males conceived humanistic gods, the Man and the Woman.[1] A society under attack from within requires updated deities, winning spirits, hence the Man and the Woman—in that order. Post-Second World War chauvinists dreamt up these novel divinities, therewith limiting the parameters of female freedom.

· · · · ·

Now, early twenty-first century, as revolutionary spirits rise in commotions of disordering opinions to drown out the Word, the proclamatory voice of the LORD God penetrates the fornicative densities.

He spoke and speaks clearly.

On the day for creating human beings, the Creator God registered the *very good* of the Genesis 1–2 history; in and for the continuance of this history, he made *submission* the unique rule—the man submissive to him, the LORD, and accountable for the woman, the woman accountable to the LORD and submissive to the man. In terms of humanity, the man and the woman stood as equals in the presence of the Creator God, the man no more human than the woman and the woman no less human than the man. Only in terms of responsibility the LORD of all creation differentiated the two; he mandated leadership, headship, to the man and subordination to the woman. Key words as submission and subordination revealed forever a crucial aspect of the Faith—believing and living also applied to the intimacies of human sexuality. The Creator God commanded the man to masculinity, submission to him, and the woman to femininity, assistance to the man in populating the world, Eden first. As the man in masculinity submitted himself to headship and the woman in femininity gave herself to the man, the two bonded in the wonder of marital union, which union Adam's fall into sin disturbed to the core. Because of the historical moment of Genesis 3:1–7, sinfulness perverted human sexuality.

As sinfulness warped male/female sexuality, the LORD God throughout the subsequent history recreated its purposefulness in order to glorify him and to mature believers in the goal of sexual bonding through submission to the Scriptures.

1. For development of this idolic tradition, pp. 92–93.

PREFACE

. . . . .

Masculinity and Femininity catalogues designs in human sexuality, the LORD God's law of sexual intimacy against laws of carnal perversion. The LORD's law of sexual intimacy applies first to all whom he draws into the Church. And second, all outside the Church, to escape miseries of brokenness, do well to submit to this law.

TH

Acknowledgments

In a way, *Masculinity and Femininity* continues *Covenant Bonds: Fundamentals of Marriage and Family,* 2011, a work my wife and I published on the Internet.

I dedicate *Masculinity and Femininity* to Rev. Dr. W. Koopmans, erudite Old Testament scholar, who over decades of ministry generated respect for the pastorate.

Masculinity and Femininity comes with the spousal *imprimatur* of Bible-reading Jayne Hoogsteen.

Since the publication of *The Tradition of the Elders,* my respect grows for the editorial staff at Wipf and Stock, Publishers.

Deformation Of Intimate Designs

AT CREATING THE HUMAN originals, the Creator God built in the male and female stabilizers, masculinity and femininity. With masculinity and femininity forever situated in respective hearts, he called the man and the woman to submission for populating the earth, thus magnifying him, the Creator God.

THE RISE OF SEXUAL INTIMACIES

Genesis 1:1—2:25

On Day Six, the Creator God crowned the created order with the innovative people-making word.

> Let us make man in our image, after our likeness. And let them have dominion over the fish of the sea and over the birds of the heavens and over the livestock and over all the earth and over every creeping thing that creeps on the earth.

> So God created man in his own image,
> in the image of God he created him;
> male and female he created them.
> Genesis 1:26–27

When God created man, he made him in the likeness of God. Male and female he created them, and he blessed them and named them [adam = human beings] when they were created. Genesis 5:1b–2

Image and likeness made first of all the man a ruler. As the LORD God ruled heaven and earth sovereignly, the man governed representatively, in the name of the Creator LORD.

At completing the initial creation, the Creator God, the LORD God, the LORD mandated the man and the woman with the primary obligation, to people the earth. Genesis 1:28, "Be fruitful and multiply and fill the earth and subdue it and reign over the fish of the sea and over the birds of the heavens and over every living thing that moves on the earth." Herewith then the man and the woman entered into the heart of marital intimacies.

. . . . .

As the man faced the headship mandate, the naming of and the ruling over the animals, the Creator God *discovered* that the man required assistance to populate Eden, to say nothing of peopling the earth. At granting the man the helper capable of the procreative directive, the LORD God created the first woman, a work as resourcefully complex as the making of the man, the two equal in personhood.[1] Genesis 2:7, 20–22, ". . . the LORD God caused a deep sleep to fall upon the man, and while he slept took one of his ribs and closed up its place with flesh. And the rib that LORD God had taken from the man he made into a woman and brought her to the man." As the LORD God escorted the woman to the man, the man recognized her unsurpassable worth and named her with exclamatory joy.

This at last is bone of my bones and flesh of my flesh;
she shall be called Woman,
because she was taken out of Man.
Genesis 2:23

1. For *Masculinity and Femininity*, a person is a human being who consciously believes or disbelieves the Scriptures as the infallible Word of God. Before the Judge of all the earth, human beings abide as actually accountable human beings—as real men and real women.

2

At naming the Woman with this forever marital vow, the man leading, the two bowed into the one-flesh union, the amazing intimacy at the heart of the marriage bond. And distinct from male masculinity, the woman in her femininity, amidst the affections and familiarities of the marital institution, submitted to assist him in the primary imperative. With the multifaceted stabilizers mutually respected and esteemed, the man and the woman of the beginning lived in the creativity of the marriage bond, the man leading, initiating, protecting, and owning first responsibility for the marriage, while hearing out and listening to the woman's interests and concerns for nuptial blooming.

On Day Seven, with proclamatory authority,[2] the LORD God blessed the crowning creative event, the making of the man and the woman. In this proclamation, the LORD with commanding force demarcated the eternal masculine and feminine stabilizers. He created the man in submission to him to own headship, leadership, with accompanying first accountability. And the evidence of headship? Obeying the divine commandments. By way of this submission, the first man,[3] due to his headship, determined the future of the human race, the way of the earth, indeed, of the universe, an authority impossible to overestimate.

A First Sum

For twenty-four hours, the man and the woman in the presence of the LORD God learned to know each other as persons, discovering connubiality in marital affirmation.

2. I interpret Genesis 2:4–25 as a Sabbath-day proclamation clarifying Genesis 1:26–27, explaining to the man and the woman the way of the intimate one-flesh union unique to marital bonding.

3. In the New Testament, Romans 5:14; 1 Corinthians 15:45, the apostolic author defined this man as the first Adam, Christ Jesus the second Adam.

THE FALL OF SEXUAL INTIMACIES

Genesis 3:1—Deuteronomy 34:12

Directly upon the empowerments of masculinity and femininity, the man and the woman corrupted these human stabilizers into masochist and feminist perversions, as narrated in the account of the Fall, Genesis 3:1–7. The woman, rather than helping the man to walk away from the Tree of the Knowledge of Good and Evil, assumed the agency of headship, which is feminism, and enticed the man to abdicate his masculinity.

Hence, post-lapsarian, the descendants of the man and the woman, generation upon generation, manipulated covetous masochism and equally covetous feminism, making the attributes of masculinity and femininity serve satanic ends, for the benefit of the men. From the Genesis 3:1–7 point in time and space, congenital competition between men and women broke out, converging in multiple million acts of despair and/or hope, brokenness and/or healing, hurt and/or happiness without minimizing the pain of conjugal conflicts.

1

At that excruciating point in time and space, as the creation collapsed into brokenness, the Creator God called first the Serpent to account, humiliating the pretentious Influencer.

Because you have done this,
cursed are you above all livestock and above all beasts of
the field;
on your belly you shall go,
and dust you shall eat all the days of your life.
I will put enmity between you and the woman,
and between your offspring and her offspring;
he shall bruise your head,
and you shall bruise his heel.
Genesis 3:14–15

In this manner, the LORD God superimposed upon the badly surprised Sinner utter condemnation and sent the Arch-intriguer upon his millennia-long slithering into damnation. He never escaped the consequences of devising the sinfulness of sin. In that descent, the LORD purposefully illuminated the way of fornication, an engulfing by eternal darkness.

. . . . .

Then, in that hour of fatally condemning the Serpent, the Creator God out of grace initiated the Recreation, the second creation, more glorious than the first; he reformed the two sin-enthused people for his exaltation. At the wondrous founding of the Recreation, he repositioned first the woman in her femininity. With more captivating language than in Genesis 2:24–25, the omnipotent LORD resituated her in submission to the man.

I will surely multiply your pain in childbearing;
in pain you shall bring forth children.
Your desire shall be for your husband and he shall rule
over you.
Genesis 3:16

That is, the woman's sexual yearnings refocused on marital intimacies with her husband, who, restored in headship, led anew in the peopling mandate. Now, reformed in her femininity, the LORD God had in effect recreated the woman, tasking her once more in femininity to populate Eden, and worlds beyond. Masculine Adam, in recognition of her responsibility, called Eve, Genesis 3:20, "the mother of all living," an exulting honor and a light in the darkness.

With the same grace, the LORD God recreated Adam for the masculinity of headship, making him, to provide for Eve and eventual children, work in a life-choking thorn-and-thistle garden.

Because you have listened to the voice of your wife
and have eaten of the tree of which I commanded you,
"You shall not eat of it,"
cursed is the ground because of you;

5

in pain[4] you shall eat of it all the days of your life;
thorns and thistles it shall bring forth for you;
and you shall eat of the plants of the field.
By the sweat of your face you shall eat bread,
till you return to the ground,
for out of it you were taken;
for you are dust,
and to dust you shall return.
Genesis 3:17–19

Along with harvesting sustenance for his family, the LORD commanded Adam to initiate connubial intimacies with Eve for peopling the Recreation, he with his descendants subduing the earth, making it livable and productive for all coming generations, all to glorify the Recreator. Every day the man assumed leadership, in the LORD accountable for Eve's wellbeing. And Adam knew Eve. The two in the one-flesh bond, even if impeded by bewildering masochism and feminism, entered the life of the Recreation.

2

To inform all generations of the Recreation with the goodness of grace and of the recreated masculine/feminine attributes, the LORD God *authored* the Scriptures. In the Book, among other energizing theological themes, he revealed these astonishing structures of accountability, the man to him and for the woman, the woman to him and to the man. In this recreation of masculinity and femininity, the LORD God commanded cooperation, the man leading, the woman submitting. These renormalized human basics the Church of all times and places acknowledges in the 1561 *Confession of Faith,* Article 5.

> We receive all these books, and these only, as holy and canonical, for the regulation, foundation, and confirmation of our faith. We believe without any doubt all things

---

4. The LORD created this word to describe a hurt similar to Eve's, without any unnecessary sympathy for Adam, the one mainly responsible for the Fall, Romans 5:12.

contained in them, not so much because the church re-
ceives and approves them as such, but especially because
the Holy Spirit witnesses in our hearts that they are from
God, and also because they contain the evidence of this
in themselves; for even the blind are able to perceive that
the things foretold in them are being fulfilled.

Over its many pages and throughout multiple subsequent-
to-the-Fall marital turmoilings, the LORD God exposes and
directs the admirable male and female stabilizers of masculinity
and femininity either to salvation or to condemnation, reproving
adventures with masochism and feminism as well as holding to
account every perversion of human sexuality.

3

However, major abuse of the recreated order and violent mistreat-
ment of headship had gripped Adam's eldest: he murdered Abel.
Upon this fratricide, the LORD God broke the formative covenant
community, sending Cain with a sister-wife to the first anti-
covenant community and counterculture—outside Eden, Genesis 4:17–24. In this other world of reality, anti-masculinity and
anti-femininity dominated human sexuality. One of Cain's great-
great-great-great-great-great-grandsons fathered authoritarian
Lamech[5] who publicly and proudly spurned the cooperativity of
masculine/feminine interactivity through bigamy. Arrogantly, this
Lamech exerted misogynistic control over Adah and Zillah, lest
the two oppose his paganizing masochism. In that anti-covenant
counter-culture, young men learned to exploit the irrationalities
of masochism and young women to manipulate the absurdities of
feminism. In short, the Cainites maladministered the radical opposition to the Recreation.

In apposition to Cain and the Cainite counterculture, the
Creator God established Seth to father the generations of the
Recreation.

5. The Scriptures register this Lamech, distinct from the one in Genesis
5:25, as the seventh generation from Adam over Cain.

By the end of that age, Cain's descendants had swallowed up Seth's covenant lineage. Through intermarriage, Seth's men, sons of God, bonded with Cain's women, daughters of man. As the anti-covenanters absorbed the covenanters, mighty rulers by way of violence submerged the masculine/feminine ordering of society into a massive counter-culture, which the LORD God with the global Deluge cleansed away, except for Noah's Eight, Genesis 6:1–8.

4

After the Flood, Noah's sons—Shem, Ham, and Japheth, Genesis 6:10, 10:1—fathered the new generations of the always surprising Recreation, thereby moving ahead with the peopling mandate, Genesis 9:1, 7. In an entirely different world milieu than Adam's, these three with respective wives—at the base of Mount Ararat—began subduing the earth into a people-friendly habitat to honor and glorify the LORD God.

1–4

The developing population, rebellious, rather than dispersing in deference to the divine command, chose to colonize the Mesopotamian Plain of Shinar, Genesis 11:1–7, to build an immense tower. Instead of obediently trusting the LORD God and accomplishing the Genesis 9:1, 7 population dictate, the men, taking the women and the children down with them, invented religiosity in opposition to the Religion. In that religiosity, the plain-dwellers developed idols[6] by which to displace the LORD God. Through these man-made gods, the people perpetuated and normalized countercultural masochism, therewith to find satisfaction in sexual adventurings, whatever the consequences for the women and children.

6. On the Plain of Shinar, rather than the pre-Flood violence of mighty men, the males invented idols, the worship of which had to guarantee powers of survival and mastery in the earth.

With an emphasis on Shem's descendants, Genesis 11:10–26, God sent those revolutionaries away from the Plain of Shinar to honor the multiplication rule by scattering all to the four winds and pre-ordained habitats. Those people, following gods and goddesses depicted as sexualized men and women, birds, animals, or creeping creatures henceforth idealized insularity from the LORD God's will. Bound to idolatrous attachments, the Recreation's covenant community disappeared under welters of counter-cultural religiosity.

2–4

Out of the exponentially multiplying descendants of the Semite Shem, the LORD drew the still wandering Abram into Canaan, Genesis 12:1–3, to create anew the Recreation's covenant community. Abram and Sarai, impatient with the promise of a son, initiated a bigamous adventure with a servant girl, Hagar, Genesis 16:1–16, who bore Ishmael. After this anti-masculine and anti-feminine diversion from the divinely evolving covenant course of marital history, the LORD God granted Abraham and Sarah Isaac, Genesis 18:14, 21:1–7. In the next covenant generation, he blessed Isaac and Rebekah with Esau and Jacob, Genesis 25:19–26.

Esau's descendants blended in with Ishmael's offspring. This anti-covenantal and countercultural civilization interacted with other idolatrous colonies of anti-Semitic peoples to counterbalance and devastate the Recreation. From Mount Seir, Esau's descendants with neighboring countries kept the multiplication mandate in masochistic and feministic ways, following this patriarch's polygamous/polyamorous example, Genesis 32:3, in the process to overwhelm the seed of the woman manifested through Isaac's Jacob.

3–4

Continuing the covenantal and cultural integrity of the Recreation, upon the Genesis 17:1–14 reformation, the LORD God transferred the masculine leadership from Isaac to Jacob/Israel to Judah, Genesis 44:32, 49:8–12, in which the women served the men beyond the mandated population increase; they managed households, engaged the community, and upheld the reputation of respective husbands.

For the covenant orientation, the LORD God revealed Israel's awing deep-seatedness in eternity.

> For you are a people holy to the LORD your God. The LORD your God has chosen you to be a people for his treasured possession, out of all the peoples who are on the face of the earth. It was not because you were more in number than any other people that the LORD set his love on you and chose you, for you were the fewest of all people, but it was because the LORD loves you and is keeping the oath that he swore to your fathers, that the LORD has brought you out with a mighty hand and redeemed you from the house of slavery, from the hand of Pharaoh king of Egypt. Know therefore that the LORD your God is God, the faithful God who keeps covenant and steadfast love with those who love him and keep his commandments, to a thousand generations, and repays to their face those who hate him, by destroying them. He will not be slack with one who hates him. He will repay him to his face. You shall therefore be careful to do the commandment and the statutes and the rules that I command you today. Deuteronomy 7:6–11

For the beneficial order of the expanding covenant nation, the LORD incorporated Jethro's legal proposal, Exodus 18:13–23; Deuteronomy 1:9–18, and ensured in all Israel the life worth living.

Hence, beginning once more with Abraham, the LORD God, through the headship of masculinity and the submission of femininity, realized his fascinating imperative for the earth in respective covenant families and tribal assemblies, the women up-holding the men in relevant offices.

4-4

Throughout the Pentateuchal, the Genesis-Deuteronomy, history thus far, the covenant LORD held the males accountable for the malignities of masochism—Adam for the original sin, Romans 5:12, Cain for murder, Genesis 4:8, Noah for drunkenness, Genesis 9:21, Ham and Canaan for mockery, Genesis 9:25, Israelite men for rebellion, Numbers 14:1–12, 39–44; Deuteronomy 1:34–40, a man for blasphemy, Numbers 15:32–36, Moses for disobedience, Numbers 20:10–13, 27:14; Deuteronomy 3:23–29, Nadab and Abihu for sacrilege, Leviticus 10:1–3, Korah, Dathan, and Abiram for revolution, Numbers 16:1–50, Israel for murmuring, Numbers 11:31–35, 32:10–15, the men of Sodom for homosexuality, Genesis 19:4–11; 2 Peter 2:10; Jude 7; etc.

In the development of the Pentateuch, Moses mentioned only Eve's deceit, Genesis 3:1–7; 1 Timothy 2:14, Sarah's disdain for the LORD's progeny promise, Genesis 18:12, Miriam's rebelling against Moses' leadership, Numbers 12:10–13, and Tamar's prostitution, Genesis 38:13–19, each happening expressive of feminism. Ordinarily, however, according to the order of masculinity, the LORD concentrated insubordination and its results on the men.

Certainly, everyone who broke with the headship structuring, women as well as men, invoked its penalties, visibly assuming appropriate punishments and serving as forewarnings. The LORD God willed to purge evil from Israel. Deuteronomy 19:20, "And the rest will hear and fear, and shall never again commit any such evil among you." Always, Israel's God detained primarily the men in terms of accountability for misaligning and ruining headship.

According to Genesis-Deuteronomy, the LORD God erected and maintained the foundational covenant standards for masculinity and femininity, severely repressing masochism and feminism.

The adjudication of Zelophehad's daughters marked out the freedom of Israelite women with respect to conjugal unions. Numbers 26:33, 36:6–7, "Let them marry whom they think best, only they shall marry within the clan of the tribe of their father. The inheritance of the people of Israel shall not be transferred from one tribe to another, for every one of the people of Israel shall hold on to the inheritance of the tribe of his fathers." Joshua 17:3–6. This wonderful freedom over against pagan predilections for arranged marriages prevailed throughout Israel.

Moreover, in Israel's conjugal structuring, brides' prices and dowries worked out economic stability for newly-weds. A prospective groom provided his bride's price, a sum of money or an object of value, for safekeeping to an authority figure, the fiancée's father or a brother, Exodus 21:7–11, 22:17. This remarkable shekel-presentation protected the young woman from insolvency in case the groom died before the wedding or reneged on his commitment. In either situation, through the betrothal, her family and neighbors considered her a married woman. The bride's price then provided a livelihood for the young woman in readjusting her life. At the wedding, the bride presented her husband with a dowry. Both objects of value provided the young couple with economic solvency early in married life.

By purchasing Naomi's land in accordance with the Leviticus 25:25–28 stipulations, Boaz acquired its crops until the next Jubilee year. This money, as bride's price, provided Naomi and Ruth living stability and gave Ruth, as inheritor of the land, a dowry.

Genesis-Deuteronomy men and women by and large made credible choices. The one-flesh union of Abram and Sarai, for instance, reflected a heart commitment stimulating emulation. The marriage of Isaac and Rebekah, Genesis 24:1–67, promised long-running hopes of unity and permanence. And the Boaz-Ruth bonding reflected the wonder of divine leading. These marital unions respected human sexuality in male/female bonding, which revelations of the human spirit accentuated the love of divine providence.

6

Within the Pentateuchal boundaries, the LORD God erected barriers that forbad transgressing the conjugality of marriage in order to hold Israel to the high road of accountability, masculinity for the men and femininity for the women. For God punished sexual sins and sinners commensurate with other types of iniquity. Every transgression and transgressor identified by the Ten Commandments, specifically now the Seventh, came to a day of reckoning. Therefore all who "chose" carnal perversities rued the consequences that simultaneously functioned as forewarnings in the social surround. The LORD God never tolerated sexual arrangements at odds with Seventh Commandment, whatever the excuses; alternative one-flesh unions found eventual repercussions. Only life-long male/female marriages duly fulfilled the Genesis 1:28 peopling mandate.

1–2

Lamech's bigamy, Genesis 5:19–24, Abram's adultery, Genesis 16:1–16, Jacob's bigamy, Genesis 29:31–35, then polygamy/polyamory, Genesis 30:1–24, Reuben's incest, Genesis 35:22, 49:4; 1 Chronicles 5:1, and Judah's incest, Genesis 38:12–19; 1 Chronicles 2:4, transgressed the ordained way of procreation, the penalties dire.

2–2

With these examples of prohibited pleasures and means of procreation, the LORD God enacted laws forbidding bigamous and polygamous/polyamorous unions. A man with a daughter and her mother, Leviticus 20:14, "If a man takes a woman and her mother also, it is depravity; he and they shall be burned with fire, that there may be no depravity among you." A bigamous man, Exodus 21:10, "If he takes another wife to himself, he shall not diminish her food, her clothing, or her marital rights." A bigamous man, Deuteronomy 21:15–17, "If a man has two wives, the one loved and the other unloved, and both the loved and the unloved have borne him children, and if the firstborn son belongs to the unloved, then on the day he assigns his possessions as an inheritance to his sons, he may not treat the son of the loved as the firstborn in preference to the son of the unloved, who is the firstborn, but he shall acknowledge the firstborn, the son of the unloved, by giving him a double portion of all that he has, for he is the firstfruits of his strength. The [primogeniture] of the firstborn is his." Bigamous and polygamous marriages, whatever animosities in a household, never lawfully excused abuse of marital bonds.

The LORD God applied the death penalty to homosexuality. Leviticus 18:22, "You shall not lie with a male as with a woman; it is abomination." Leviticus 20:13, "If a man lies with a male as with a woman, both of them shall have committed an abomination; they shall surely be put to death; their blood is upon them." Cross-dressing too earned condemnation, Deuteronomy 22:5. Power centers of homosexuality, also homosexualism, presented less than enticing reckonings for men and for women.

Upon incest too the LORD imposed severe penalties. By way of Leviticus 18:1–18, he condemned incestuous sexuality. "None of you shall approach any one of his close relatives to uncover nakedness. I am the LORD. You shall not uncover the nakedness of your father, which is the nakedness of your mother; you shall not uncover her nakedness. You shall not uncover the nakedness of your father's wife; it is your father's nakedness. You shall not uncover the nakedness of your sister, your father's daughter or your mother's daughter; whether brought up in the family or in another home. You shall not uncover the nakedness of your son's daughter or of your daughter or of your daughter's daughter; for their nakedness is your nakedness. You shall not uncover the nakedness of your father's wife's daughter brought up in your father's family, since she is your sister. You shall not uncover the nakedness of your father's sister; she is your father's relative.[7] You shall not uncover the nakedness of your mother's sister, for she is your mother's relative. You shall not uncover the nakedness of your father's brother; that is, you shall not approach his wife; she is your aunt. You shall not uncover the nakedness of your daughter-in-law; she is your son's wife, you shall not uncover her nakedness. You shall not uncover the nakedness of your brother's wife; it is your brother's nakedness. You shall not uncover the nakedness of a woman and of her daughter, and you shall not take your son's daughter or her daughter's daughter to uncover her nakedness; they are relatives; it is depravity. And you shall not take a woman as a rival wife to her sister; uncovering her nakedness while her sister is still alive." Thus the LORD God proscribed consanguine conflict in marital unions.

Moreover, the LORD God emphatically repeated incestuous prohibitions. Leviticus 20:11–12, "If a man lies with his father's wife, he has uncovered his father's nakedness; both of them shall surely be put to death; their blood is upon them. If a man lies with his daughter-in-law, both of them shall surely be put to death; they have committed perversion; their blood is upon them." Leviticus 20:17, "If a man takes his sister, a daughter of his father or a daughter of his mother, and sees her nakedness, and she sees his nakedness, it is a disgrace, and they shall be cut off in the sight of the children of their people. He has uncovered his sister's nakedness, and he shall bear his iniquity." Leviticus 20:19–21, "You shall not uncover the nakedness of your mother's sister or of your father's sister, for that is to make naked one's relative; they shall bear their iniquity. If a man lies with his uncle's wife, he has uncovered his uncle's nakedness; they shall bear their sin; they shall die childless. If a man takes his brother's wife, it is impurity. He has uncovered his brother's nakedness; they shall die childless." Deuteronomy 22:30, "A man shall not take his father's wife, so that he does not uncover his father's nakedness." Deuteronomy 27:20a, "Cursed be anyone who lies with his father's wife, because he has uncovered his father's nakedness." Deuteronomy 27:22a, "Cursed be anyone

---

7. Exodus 6:20, Amram married his father's sister, Jochebed.

who lies with his sister, whether the daughter of his father or the daughter of his mother." Deuteronomy 27:23a, "Cursed be anyone who lies with his mother-in-law." The LORD God willed to purge incestuous abominations from among his people and uphold the wholesomeness of male/female connubiality. Leviticus 18:24–30,

> Do not make yourselves unclean by any of these things, for by all these the nations I am driving out before you have become unclean, and the land became unclean, so that I punished its iniquity, and the land vomited out its inhabitants. But you shall keep my statutes and my rules and do none of these abominations, either the native or the stranger who sojourns among you (for the people of the land, who were before you, did all these abominations, so that the land became unclean), lest the land vomit you out when you make it unclean, as it vomited out the nation that was before you. For everyone who does any of these abominations, the persons who do them shall be cut off from among their people. So keep my charge never to practice any of these abominable customs that were practiced before you, and never to make yourselves unclean by them: I am the LORD your God.

Throughout Israel, the resolute LORD God demanded holiness in human sexuality, in which freedom the people thankfully acknowledged the grace of salvation.

The LORD God enacted the death penalty upon adultery; such is the force of Exodus 20:14; Deuteronomy 5:18, "*You shall not commit adultery.*" Leviticus 18:20, "And you shall not lie sexually with your neighbor's wife and so make yourself unclean with her." Leviticus 20:10, "If a man commits adultery with the wife of his neighbor, both the adulterer and the adulteress shall surely be put to death." Deuteronomy 22:22, "If a man is found lying with the wife of another man, both of them shall die, the man who lay with the woman, and the woman. So you shall purge evil from Israel." And one more, Deuteronomy 22:25, ". . . if in the open country a man meets a young woman who is betrothed, and the man seizes her and lies with her, then only the man who lay with her shall die. But you shall do nothing to the young woman; she has committed no offense punishable by death. . . . because he met her in the open country, and though the betrothed young woman cried for help there was no one to rescue her." In this manner, too, the LORD eradicated every evil coupling from among his people.

Bestiality as well lacked good judgment and merited the death penalty. Exodus 22:19, "Whoever lies with an animal shall be put to death." Leviticus 18:23, 20:15–16, "If a man lies with an animal, he shall surely be put to death, and you shall kill the animal. If a woman approaches any animal and lies with it, you shall kill the woman and the animal; they shall surely be put to death; their blood is upon them." Deuteronomy 27:21a, "Cursed be anyone who lies with any kind of animal." The LORD intended also in this matter of vital concern the holiness of his people.

Rapists summarily forfeited life. Genesis 34:1–4, 25, Shechem's rape of Dinah, Jacob's daughter, escalated into multiple violent deaths. Deuteronomy 22:23–27, "If there is a betrothed virgin, and a man meets her in the city and lies with her, then you shall bring both out to the gate of that city, and you shall stone them to death with stones, the young woman because she did not cry for help though she was in the city, and the man because he violated his neighbor's wife. So you shall purge the evil from your midst." In one rape case, the LORD granted exception to the death penalty. Deuteronomy 22:28–29, "If a man meets a virgin who is not betrothed, and seizes her and lies with her, and they are found, then the man who lay with her shall give to the father of the young woman [the bride's price], and she shall be his wife, because he violated her. He shall not divorce her all his days." Rape too had its unsavory consequences.

The LORD God strictly forbad prostitution. Leviticus 19:29, "Do not profane your daughter by making her a prostitute, lest the land fall into prostitution and the land become full of depravity." Deuteronomy 23:17, "None of the daughters of Israel shall be a cult prostitute." This anti-prostitution command applied to men too. Deuteronomy 23:17–18, ". . . none of the sons of Israel shall be a cult prostitute. You shall not bring the fee of a prostitute or the wages of a dog into the house of the LORD your God in payment for any vow, for both of these are an abomination to the LORD your God." Anyone complicit in prostitution paid the price.

Norm-breaking whoring also warranted death. Exodus 34:15–16, ". . . (for you shall worship no other god, for the LORD, whose name is Jealous, is a jealous God), lest you make a covenant with the inhabitants of the land, and when they whore after their gods and sacrifice to their gods and you are invited to eat of his sacrifice, and you take of their daughters for your sons, and their daughters whore after their gods and make your sons whore after their gods." Leviticus 21:9; Numbers 25:1–5, "While Israel lived in Shittim, the people began to whore with the daughters of Moab. These invited the people to the sacrifices of their gods. So Israel yoked himself to Baal of Peor. And the anger of the LORD was kindled against Israel. And the LORD said to Moses, 'Take all the chiefs of the people and hang them in the sun before the LORD, that the fierce anger of the LORD may turn away from Israel.' And Moses said to the judges of Israel, 'Each of you kill those of his men who have yoked themselves to Baal of Peor.'" Leviticus 20:22–26; Numbers 25:6–9; Deuteronomy 22:13–21; Joshua 22:17. Instant justice concluded that whoring event.

Divorce and remarriage came under worrying judgment. Deuteronomy 24:1–5, "When a man takes a wife and marries her, if then she finds no favor in his eyes because he has found some indecency in her, and he writes her a certificate of divorce and puts it in her hand and sends her out of his house, and she departs from his house, and if she goes and becomes another man's wife, and the latter man hates her and writes her a certificate of divorce and puts it in her hand and sends her out of his house, or if the latter man dies, who took her to be his wife, then her former husband, who sent her away, may not take her again to be his wife, after she has been defiled, for that is an abomination before the LORD. And you shall not bring sin upon the land that the LORD your God is giving you for an inheritance." The LORD God had no patience with Is-raelite men who misused the marital institution for covetous ends.

The LORD revealed the same impatience with mismanage-ment of levirate marriages. Deuteronomy 25:5–10, "If brothers dwell together, and one of them dies and has no son, the wife of the dead man shall not be married outside the family to a stranger. Her husband's brother shall go in to her and shall take her as his wife and perform the duty of a husband's brother to her. And the first son whom she bears shall succeed to the name of his dead brother, that his name may not be blotted out of Israel. And if the man does not wish to take his brother's wife, then his brother's wife shall go up to the gate to the elders and say, 'My husband's brother refuses to perpetuate his brother's name in Israel; he will not perform the duty of a husband's brother to me.' Then the elders of the city shall call him and speak to him, and if he persists, saying 'I do not wish to take her,' then his brother's wife shall go up to him in the presence of the elders and pull his sandal off his foot and spit in his face. And she shall answer and say, 'So shall it be done to the man who does not build up his brother's house.' And the name of his house shall be called in Israel, 'The house of him who had his sandal pulled off.'" Levirate unions prevented sufferings of widowhood and sanctioned perpetuation of genealogies.

The LORD God also barred intermarrying. Genesis 6:1–4 records the ruinous blending of Seth's seed with that of Cain's. Exodus 34:15–16; Deuteronomy 7:3–4, "You shall not intermarry with [the indigenous populations], giving your daughters to their sons or taking their daughters for your sons, for they would turn away your sons from following me, to serve other gods. Then the anger of the LORD would be kindled against you, and he would destroy you quickly." With enough sinfulness rampant in the covenant community, inviting more from the outside complicated Israel's carnal immoralities unnecessarily.

To supplant the commanded way of masculinity and femininity with sexual perversions ran contrary to the intents of marital intimacies. The LORD God decreed holiness for the marriage order. Leviticus 18:24–30, specifically 18:30, "So keep my charge never to practice any of these abominable customs that were practiced before you, and never to make yourselves unclean by them: I am the LORD your God." Leviticus 20:23; Numbers 33:55–56, at Israel's possession of Canaan, "But if you do not drive out the inhabitants of the land from before you, then those of them whom you let remain shall be as barbs in your eyes and thorns in your sides, and they shall trouble you in the land where you dwell. And I will do to you as I thought to do to them." In short, Leviticus 19:2, "You shall be holy, for I the LORD your God am holy." Joseph, son of Jacob, exemplified this holiness by warding off the allures of Potiphar's wife, Genesis 39:1–18.

7

Inside the covenant community, the men in the convictions of masculinity took astounding initiatives of responsibility, acknowledging in submission before the LORD God the driving force of first accountability for marriages and family unions.

Outside the covenant community, the provocations of masochism deprecated marital integrity; with no criterion other than covetousness to direct human sexuality, every conceivable carnal travesty reared into prominence. Lamech's bigamy made its rebellious statement, along with initial evidence of misogyny, Genesis 4:19, he bidding Adah and Zillah into compliance. The Pharaoh of Genesis 12:15, the Abimelech of Genesis 20:2, and no doubt the Abimelech of Genesis 26:1 owned harems; these polygamous/polyamorous rulers took in unmarried women as they pleased.

Those harem-owners reflected one commendable light: they feared adultery. The Pharaoh of Genesis 12:19, the Abimelech of Genesis 20:3, and the other Abimelech too, Genesis 26:10, knew an inner aversion to taking another man's wife sexually. They feared transgressing the marital order of the beginning.

Esau, in revenge mode, chose bigamy, Genesis 26:34–35, then polygamy, Genesis 28:8–9, multiplying anti-covenant peoples. Sodom as a whole submitted to lusts of sodomy, Genesis 19:4–11; 2 Peter 2:10; Jude 7. Lot's daughters plotted incest, Genesis 19:30–38, turning out hateful Moabites and Ammonites. The LORD God, in the astute making of history, drew a regulatory line between Israel and the nations. On the dark side of that antithesis no criterion other than masochistic covetousness dominated human sexuality.

To make the dividing-line apparent, the LORD God created a hard and fast antithesis between his people and the other nations, lest the others worsen Israel's abuses of masculinity and femininity.

A Second Sum

Before advancing with the masculine and feminine attributes, several piquant observations rise to attention:

One. Scriptures named only some women—Adam's Eve, Lamech's Adah and Zillah, Genesis 4:19; Nahor's Milcah, Genesis 11:29; Abram/Abraham's Sarai/Sarah, Genesis 17:5, 15; Isaac's Rebekah, Genesis 24:15; Jacob's Leah and Rachel, Genesis 29:15–30, then Bilhah, Genesis 30:4, and Zilpah, Genesis 30:9; Esau's Judith and Basemath, Genesis 26:34–35, then Mahalath, Genesis 28:9; Judah's Bathshua, Genesis 38:1–5; 1 Chronicles 2:3; Joseph's Asenath, Genesis 41:45; Moses' Zipporah, Exodus 2:21; Aaron's Elisheba, Exodus 6:23; Amram's, Jochebed, Exodus 6:20; Numbers 26:59. Others remained unnamed—Cain's, Seth's, Noah's, Shem's, Ham's, Japheth's wives and those of Jacob's sons, except Judah's.

Two. Upon repeating the multiplication command, Genesis 9:1, 7, Noah's sons fathered the new generations of the Recreation, Genesis 10:1–32, 11:10–26. Abraham's Sarah bore one son, Isaac, Isaac's Rebekah bore two sons, Esau and Jacob, Lot's wife two daughters, Genesis 19:8, Jacob's four wives thirteen children, Genesis 35:23–25, Amram's Jochebed three (Aaron, Moses, and Miriam, Exodus 6:20; Numbers 12:1), the priest of Midian's wife seven daughters, Exodus 2:16, Moses's Zipporah two sons, Exodus 2:22, 4:20, and Aaron's Elisheba four sons (Nadab, Abihu, Eleazar, and Ithamar), Exodus 6:23. All in all, Israel multiplied, Exodus 1:9; Deuteronomy 1:10–11.

Three. Willful anti-masculinity and anti-femininity plagued also the covenant community. Whatever the fleeting pleasures and satisfactions: adultery, bigamy, polygamy/polyamory, incest, and rape blackened the LORD's people with carnal sins. Because of sinning, Abraham had to send his firstborn, Ishmael off into the wilderness. Hagar experienced rough living under Sarai/

Sarah's command and later, with Ishmael, a wilderness existence. Jacob disinherited his firstborn for incest, Genesis 35:22, 49:3–4; Deuteronomy 33:6. Judah, guilty of incest and Tamar of prostitution, faced shame, Genesis 38:1–30. To make matters worse, Ishmael's descendants and the offspring of Abraham's concubines, Genesis 25:1–6, joined anti-covenant civilizations oppressive of Israel. Esau's seed too blended in with the covenant opponents. The continuing friction between Leah and Rachel soured Jacob's life and the budding covenant community. This is to say, the LORD's hand lay heavy upon anti-masculine and anti-feminine sexual adventurism; distortions of the marital order, never victimless sins, multiplied painful punishments on inescapable days of reckoning.

. . . . .

Despite the then divisive masochistic and feministic adventuring, the LORD God willed growth in the living fabric of the covenant community; in the midst of transnational anti-covenantalism, he blessed his people.

> And if you faithfully obey the voice of the LORD your God, being careful to do all his commandments that I command you today, the LORD your God will set you high above all the nations of the earth. And all these blessings shall come upon you and overtake you, if you obey the voice of the LORD your God. Blessed shall you be in the city, and blessed shall you be in the field. Blessed shall be the fruit of your womb and the fruit of your ground and the fruit of your cattle, the increase of your herds and the young of your flock. Blessed shall be your basket and your kneading bowl. Blessed shall you be when you come in, and blessed shall you be when you go out. Leviticus 26:3–13; Deuteronomy 28:1–5

The eventuality of the Incarnation moved the LORD God to bless Israel; he commanded his people to embody the Genesis 3:14–15 hope, indefatigable source of great blessings.

The LORD throughout Moses' Pentateuch drew the dividing-line and affixed its boundary: on the surprising light side, he revealed the sexual laws emanating gratitude for salvation and on the dark side he specified condemnable anti-masculine and anti-feminine behaviors. On every page, God revealed that masculinity and femininity constitute matters of the heart evident in grooming as well as in cares for body and mind. He created and recreated the submissive cores of manhood and womanhood, with all attention on the Adam/Eve marital structure as the sole God-willed male/female sexual connective in every generation.

THE ABUSE OF SEXUAL INTIMACIES

Joshua 1:1—Esther 10:3

Abuse of masculinity, masochism, and misuse of femininity, feminism, marked Israel also in the other historical Old Testament books; Israel's inner disposition to amorphous sexual depravity predisposed the covenant people to copy the carnal immoralities of the nations.

1

At Israel's entry into the Promised Land, the incorruptible LORD God lifted high the covenant nation's sexual wholesomeness, commanding Joshua (with assistants) to circumcise all males; by this painful rite, he instructed the men in headship to follow Abraham's example in procreativity with respective wives only.

> At that time the LORD said to Joshua, "Make flint knives and circumcise the sons of Israel a second time."[8] So Joshua made flint knives and circumcised the sons of Israel at Gibeath-haaraloth. And this is the reason why Joshua circumcised them: all the males of the people who came out of Egypt, all the men of war, had died in the wilderness on the way after they had come out of Egypt. Though all the people who came out had been

---

8. The "first" circumcision occurred at birth, on the eight day. The "second" happened to the new generation born during the forty years of desert journeying.

circumcised, yet all the people who were born on the way in the wilderness after they had come out of Egypt had not been circumcised. Joshua 5:3–5

The circumcision cut thus affirmed what the LORD God, after the Genesis 16:1–16 Hagar-affair, had mandated Abram/Abraham. Genesis 17:10, "This is my covenant, which you shall keep between me and you and your offspring after you: Every male among you shall be circumcised." Thereby Israelite males owned first responsibility for the sexual intimacies of marital fidelity in order to populate Canaan; the LORD proscribed every carnal infidelity. Even more, the foundational Pentateuch prohibited throughout the generations all adventuring with human sexuality.

2

For the Joshua 1:1— Samuel 31:13 metanarrative, the LORD confirmed the way of marital purity by affirming the blessings and curses intrinsic to the Mosaic covenant; by its forthtelling, the curses echoed and reechoed between Mount Gerizim and Mount Gebal.

> Deuteronomy 27:16a, "Cursed be anyone who dishonors his father or his mother."
> Deuteronomy 27:20a, "Cursed be anyone who lies with his father's wife, because he has uncovered his nakedness."
> Deuteronomy 27:21a, "Cursed be anyone who lies with any kind of animal."
> Deuteronomy 27:22a, "Curse be anyone who lies with his sister, whether the daughter of his father or the daughter of his mother."
> Deuteronomy 27:23a, "Cursed be anyone who lies with his mother-in-law."
> Joshua 8:30–35

In an adventurous market place of religiosities, these and other carnal sins condemned not only the individuals involved, the nation as whole too, for permitting such carnality to happen and perpetuate. The curses stipulated inappropriate ways for sexual intimacy and/or procreation. And Israel failed, first, by inadequately cleansing the land of indigenous population, and, second, by entering into the divinely condemned carnal life choices. Therefore, the angel of the LORD connected to Israel, Judges 2:3, "So now I say, 'I will not drive them out before you, but they shall become thorns in your sides, and their gods shall be a snare to you.'" The proximity of indigenous neighbors contaminated Israel's willingness to erotic sinning with its momentary gratifications; generation after generation, the nation tilted into sexual adventurisms.

3

Prostitution gained entry into Israel.[9] Jephthah, a prostitute's son, before assuming leadership, lived as an issue of Israel's low moral standards. Samson took advantage of Philistine prostitution to gratify sexual appetites—one in Gaza, another, Delilah, in the Valley of Sorek, Judges 16:4–22. Anti-masculine men took matters into hand as they pleased. The LORD God condemned those weak Israelite males for seeking and buying illicit pleasures.

In Israel, he barred the covenant men from feministic misuse. Deuteronomy 23:17a, "None of the daughters of Israel shall be a cult prostitute." This command prohibited female prostitution in every way.

Abuse of masculinity increased with institutionalized male cult prostitution copied from perversities operative in pagan temples, which deviancy broke with Deuteronomy 23:17b, ". . . none of the sons of Israel shall be a cult prostitute." Whatever permissiveness troubled indigenous populations, the LORD God rigorously forbad such inappropriate physical intimacies. Yet male prostitution for a homosexual clientele took hold. First Kings 14:24, ". . . and there were also male cult prostitutes in the land."

9. Rahab's prostitution indicated a normalcy throughout Canaan's indigenous populations, Joshua 2:1–21, 6:17, 22–23, 25. Her contact with Israel brought about conversion; the LORD God saved her from condemnation, by grace transforming her into a mother in Israel. Matthew 1:5; James 2:25.

They did according to all the abominations of the nations that the LORD drove out before the people of Israel." Second Kings 8:16–19. Still, faithful kings, Davidides, condemned this carnal deviation. First Kings 15:12, 22:46; 2 Kings 23:7, "And [Josiah] broke down the houses of the male cult prostitutes who were in the house of the LORD, where the women wove hangings for the Asherah." Stimulated by outside sources, male and female prostitution became deeply entrenched in impressionable Israel, thereby defining periods of easy corruptibility.

4

Israel opened to whoring. The Author recorded this idolatrous immorality in Numbers 25:1–5; such degenerate festivities crossed the Exodus 34:15–16 boundaries, the legitimacy of which profound, ". . . lest you make a covenant with the inhabitants of the land, and when they whore after their gods and sacrifice to their gods and you are invited, you eat of this sacrifice, and you take of their daughters for your sons, and their daughters whore after their gods and make your sons whore after their gods." Neither is this the way of male and female stabilizers ensuring marital wholeness. Of this whoring, Judges 2:11–14 described a descent into immoralities to accent Israel's instability. "And the people of Israel did what was evil in the sight of the LORD and served the Baals. And they abandoned the LORD, the God of their fathers, who had brought them out of the land of Egypt. They went after other gods, from among the gods of the peoples who were around them, and bowed down to them. And they provoked the LORD to anger. They abandoned the LORD and served the Baals and the Asheroth. So the anger of the LORD was kindled against Israel, and he gave them over to plunderers, who plundered them. And he sold them into the hand of their surrounding enemies, so that they could no longer withstand their enemies." Unambiguously, Judges 2:17, "Yet they did not listen to their judges, for they whored after other gods and bowed down to them. They soon turned aside from the way in which their fathers had walked, who had obeyed the commandments of the LORD, and they did not do so." In those paganized festivities, Israel too disregarded all carnal prohibitions, thus to satisfy fornicative lusts enthusiastically. In the passages of time, contempt for these covenant laws pertaining to marital fidelity worsened. Judges 3:7, "And the people of Israel did what was evil in the sight of the LORD. They forgot the LORD their God and served the Baals and the Asheroth." In every town, village, and hamlet, Israel worshiped these sexualized images: promptings to immoralities proved too strong. And morally insensitive and incentivized, Israel inclined to licentious satisfaction copied from native sources, which merited condemnation upon condemnation.

Rather than worship and serve the LORD God out of gratitude for the freedom of Canaan, the people of the covenant submitted inexorably to assimilative social tides as these washed over them. The charm of each Baal, a sexualized fertility/weather god, and the allure of each Asherah (plural: Asherim), a sexualized pole representative of Baal's consort, constantly stimulated pornographic images and illicit couplings. The murderous violence of the Ophrah citizens after Gideon had demolished the local Baal and cut down its Asherah, indicated the dark depths of soul controlling commonplace idolatrous whoring. Judges 6:25–27, 30, "'Then the men of the town said to [Gideon's father], 'Bring out your son, that he may die, for he has broken down the altar of Baal and cut down the Asherah beside it.'" This willingness to murder publicly exposed extents of heart-centered eeriness to which those Israelite masochists protected immorality. The ubiquity of these sexualized symbols excited male and female lusts to infidelity, destabilizing masculinity and femininity. And even Gideon failed the LORD God. Judges 8:27, ". . . Gideon made an ephod [of Midianite gold] and put it in his city, in Ophrah. And all Israel whored after it there, and it became a snare to Gideon and to his family." On the one hand, Gideon spectacularly eliminated the Midianite threat; on the other, he firmly fastened Israel in a Baal fertility cult.

In Baalism, altars and Asherim identified characteristics of place, high places, raised areas on which idolatrous whoring occurred, 1 Kings 3:2. Idolatry on these high places purposefully relegated the LORD God to Israelite sidelines even while they relished immoral sexualities that invoked condemnation upon condemnation. First Kings 14:22–23, "And Judah did what was evil in the sight of the LORD and they provoked him to jealousy with their sins that they committed, more than all their fathers had done, for they built for themselves high places and pillars and Asherim on every high hill and under every green tree." First Kings 16:31–33, ". . . [Ahab] took for his wife Jezebel the daughter of Ethbaal king of the Sidonians, and went and served Baal and worshiped him. He erected an altar for Baal in the house of Baal, which he built in Samaria. And Ahab made an Asherah. Ahab did more to provoke the LORD, the God of Israel, to anger than all the kings of Israel who were before him." Second Kings 13:6, 17:9–11, "And the people of Israel did secretly against the LORD their God things that were not right. They built for themselves high places in all their towns, from watchtower to fortified city. They set up for themselves pillars and Asherim on every high hill and under every green tree, and there they made offerings on all the high places, as the nations did whom the LORD carried away before them. And they did wicked things, provoking the LORD to anger." Second Kings 17:16, "And they abandoned all the commandments of the LORD their God, and made for themselves metal images of two calves, and they made an Asherah and worshiped all the host of heaven and served Baal." Second Kings 21:3, "For [Manasseh] rebuilt the high places that Hezekiah his father had destroyed, and he erected altars for Baal and made an Asherah, as Ahab king of Israel had done, and worshiped all the host of heaven and served them." Second Kings 21:7, "And the carved image of Asherah that [Manasseh] had made he set in the house of which the LORD said to David and to Solomon his son, 'In this house, and in Jerusalem, which I have chosen out of all the tribes of Israel, I will put my name forever.'" Second Chronicles 33:2–5. King Jehoram wrapped Judah in idolatrous whoring. Second Chronicles 21:11, "Moreover, he made high places in the hill country of Judah and led the inhabitants of Jerusalem into whoredom and made Judah go astray." Second Chronicles 28:25, "In every city of Judah [Ahaz] made high places to make offerings to other gods, provoking to anger the LORD, the God of his fathers." These kings, paganizing Davidides, increased the volatility in Israel's whoring.

Other kings, God-fearing Davidides, opposed the covenant nation's assimilation and legislated destruction of whoring structures. First Kings 15:13–14, "[Asa] also removed Maacah his mother from being queen mother because she had made an abominable image for Asherah. And Asa cut down her image and burned it at the brook Kidron. But the high places were not taken away. Nevertheless, the heart of Asa was wholly true to the LORD all his days." Second Kings 23:4, "And [Josiah] commanded Hilkiah the high priest and the priests of the second order and the keepers of the threshold to bring out of the temple of the LORD all the vessels made for Baal, for Asherah, and for all the host of heaven. He burned them outside Jerusalem in the fields of the Kidron and carried their ashes to Bethel." Second Kings 23:6, "And [Josiah] brought out the Asherah from the house of the LORD, outside Jerusalem, to the brook Kidron, and burned it at the brook Kidron and beat it to dust and cast the dust of it upon the graves of the common people."[10] Second Chronicles 31:1, ". . . all Israel who were present went out to the cities of Judah and broke in pieces the pillars and cut down the Asherim and broke down the high place and the altars throughout Judah and Benjamin, and in Ephraim and Manasseh, until they had destroyed them all. Then all the people of Israel returned to their cities, every man to his possession." Second Chronicles 34:3–4, ". . . [Josiah] began to seek the God of David his father, and in the twelfth year he began to purge Judah and Jerusalem of the high places, the Asherim, and the carved and metal images. And they chopped down the altars of the Baals in his presence, and he cut down the incense altars that stood above them. And he broke in pieces the Asherim and carved and metal images, and he made dust of them and scattered it over the graves of those who had sacrificed to them." The LORD God thus condemned the whoring committed at the high places

10. These Israelites had worshiped the now burned and disintegrated idol-images, gods unable to assist in approaching calamities.

as illegitimate means of worship and of peopling Canaan. Yet, this idolic sinfulness had deeply occupied the covenant soul, finding its resonance satisfying. In one instance, this whoring led to mass rape, Judges 19:22–26.

5

Despite Joshua's warning, Israelite men still contracted intermarriages. Joshua 23:12–13, "For if you turn back and cling to the remnant of these nations remaining among you and make marriages with them, so that you associate with them and they with you, know for certain that the LORD your God will no longer drive out these nations before you, but they shall be a snare and a trap for you, a whip on your sides and thorns in your eyes, until you perish from off this good ground that the LORD your God has given you." Israel refused to heed this prohibition. Judges 3:5–6, "So the people of Israel lived among the Canaanites, the Hittites, the Amorites, the Perizzites, the Hivites, and the Jebusites. And their daughters they took to themselves for wives, and they served their gods." Such marital bonding gave to pagans in some sense a covenant standing; for each such bonded union aligned religiously disparate families, a covenant family submitting to an idolatrous family, thus abusing masculinity and femininity. Masochistic Samson chose a Philistine woman, Judges 14:2, ". . . he came up and told his father and mother, 'I saw one of the daughters of the Philistines at Timnah. Now get her for me as my wife." Without respect for the divine commandment and Israel's integrity as the covenant people, Samson did as Samson willed, even though the LORD prohibited such bonding. Impertinent Samson chose his own way, which led to deepening hatred between Israel and the Philistines, Judges 14:1–20. The Benjamin-tribe, after internecine warring left too few women for the procreation mandate, simply kidnapped women for marital intimacies, ignoring the freedom of these women in the selection of conjugal partners, Judges 21:13–21. In that same period, Naomi's sons, Mahlon and Chilion, took Moabite wives, Ruth 1:4. Solomon, after marrying a Pharaonic daughter, intermarried multiple times with Moabite, Edomite, Sidonian, and Hittite women, adding numerous concubines from among those foreign nations, 1 Kings 11:1–3; 2 Chronicles 2:17. By erasing the divine boundaries and ignoring the LORD's proscription, Solomon set an example that brought division and death in Israel. Solomon's son, Rehoboam, followed in his father's footsteps, 2 Chronicles 11:18–21. Ezra, 9:1–15, and Nehemiah, 13:23–29, confronted multiple intermarriages in Israel. Esther too committed herself to an illegitimate marriage, to a polygamous monarch, Esther 2:15–18. Marital bonding with foreigners activated idolatry within the covenant nation.

6

In place of standard setting Adam-and-Eve marriages, Israel tolerated, if not approved, contrary to the Pentateuchal proscriptions both bigamy and polygamy/polyamory. As masculinity sagged into masochism, the pull-factor of these two sexual perversions betrayed Israel's covenant uprightness. So Elkanah's bigamy, 1 Samuel 1:2, Hannah the oppressed wife. First Chronicles 2:18 records another illegal two-wife bonding.

1–3

In the life-force of the Judges, every man doing what was right in his own eyes, polygamy's masochism appealed—Gideon's, Judges 8:30; Jair's, Judges 10:4; Ibzan's, Judges 12:9; and Abdon's, Judges 12:13—and defeated the long-term deliverances from overpowering enemies. Such Israelite leaders as these four led the way into assimilation with surrounding nations; Israel made pagan sinning its folly, *compelling* the LORD God to summon forth the other judges.

David married Saul's daughter, Michal, 1 Samuel 18:17–29. Later, while David fled for his life, Saul gave Michal to one Palti, 1 Samuel 25:44, or Paltiel, 2 Samuel 3:5. David, by marrying Abigail, 1 Samuel 25:42, committed bigamy, and then by wedding Ahinoam polygamy, 1 Samuel 28:43, 30:5, a fact restated in 2 Samuel 2:2. To make matters worse, destabilizing, masochistic David married more women, 2 Samuel 3:2–5. And in the course of stabilizing the monarchy in a human manner, he insisted on the return of Michal, 2 Samuel 3:14–16; he refused to have a king's daughter free to claim the throne.

David's adultery with Bathsheba and the murder of her husband, Uriah, broke the LORD's patience with the man, 2 Samuel 11:1–27; 1 Kings 15:5. Henceforth, lacking moral authority, the curse of the LORD rested on him. Second Samuel 12:10, "Now therefore the sword shall never depart from your house, because you have despised me and have taken the wife of Uriah the Hittite to be your wife." David could have had more wives, women who knowingly and willingly walked into harem oblivion. Thus, the LORD, 2 Samuel 12:8, "And I gave you your master's house and your master's wives into your arms and gave you the house of Israel and of Judah. And if this were too little, I would add to you as much more." By his carnal adventuring, David had to have another man's wife, which adultery bankrupted the man's moral integrity and set off violent episodes—Amnon's incestuous rape of Tamar, 2 Samuel 13:1–19; Absalom's murder of Amnon, 2 Samuel 13:23–29; Absalom's civil war to dethrone his father, 2 Samuel 15:1—18:18; warring with the Northern Tribes, 2 Samuel 20:1–22; and Adonijah's failed coups, 1 Kings 1:5–10, 2:13–25. David's sons, the one after the other, sought the Jerusalem throne. With the Bathsheba-affair, David had lost the moral authority of headship.

After marrying a Pharaoh's daughter to secure his southern border regions, 1 Kings 3:1, *wise* Solomon's masochistic covetousness knew no limits—700 wives, princesses, 1 Kings 11:3, which harem made him resemble an eastern potentate, fully in denial of the Deuteronomy 17:14–20 royal mandate. First Kings 11:4–6,

> For when Solomon was old his wives turned his heart after other gods, and his heart was not wholly true to the LORD his God, as was the heart of David his father. For Solomon went after Astoreth the goddess of the Sidonians, and after Milcom the abomination of the Ammonites. So Solomon did what was evil in the sight of the LORD and did not wholly follow the LORD, as David his father had done.

Rehoboam, Solomon's son with eighteen wives (of whom Maacha the preferred one), 2 Chronicles 11:21, and his grandson, Abijah, with fourteen wives, 2 Chronicles 13:21 too sought masochistic polyamory. In short, Solomon, Rehoboam, and Abijah's fornicative alliances led Judah down tumultuous ways of disobedience.

And then the Esther-history. When Ahasuerus' queen, Vashti, refused his command to parade her beauty before peoples and princes, she incited masochism, to compel wives to obey husbands. Esther 1:22, "[Ahasuerus] sent letters to all the royal provinces, to every province in its own script and to every people in its own language, that every man be master in his own household and speak according to the language of his people." Such anti-masculinity dishonored women.

3-3

Concubinage, adding faux wives to a harem, further multiplied carnal sinning to gain marital intimacies. Gideon supported such a woman, Judges 8:31. A Levite, of all people, took a concubine to wife, Judges 19:1. Masochistic Saul had Rizpah, 2 Samuel 3:7. David owned such women, 2 Samuel 5:13, and Solomon kept a bevy of 300, 1 Kings 11:3.

In the 1 Chronicles genealogies, the author remembered Abraham's Kenturah, 1:32; Genesis 25:1–6, Caleph's Ephah, 2:46, and Maacah, 2:48, and Rehoboam's sixty, 2 Chronicles 11:21. Since concubinage caricatured the Adam-and-Eve marital standard, it remained outside the divinely created bounds.

The LORD God never permitted bigamy, polygamy/polyamory, and concubinage as procreative ways, nor tolerated such paganized carnal intimacies in the Church. All of the covenant community, who prioritized such sexual satisfactions gave in to perverse feelings and had to account for these transgressions in days of reckoning—as the Assyrian and Babylonian invasions.

A Third Sum

The LORD God condemned sexual adventuring throughout Joshua 1:1—Esther 10:3, which included rape, Deuteronomy 22:25, incest, 1 Chronicles 2:24; Leviticus 18:8, and mass kidnappings by Benjamin-men, Judges 21:16–24; these added to the fornicative fracturing of the Law, that is, broken gratitude. Throughout, consistently, the LORD God upheld the one-flesh male/female life of marveling intimacies.

THE FOLLY OF SEXUAL PERVERSITY

Old Testament's wisdom literature—Job, the Psalms, Proverbs, Ecclesiastes, and the Song of Solomon—sidelines fools who casually and willfully transgress human sexuality for perverse intimacies; they grasp at condemnation.

1

Job, wise in masculinity, exemplified a procreator's love for his wife only and a startling protector's care for his ten children. He presented them sacrificially before the LORD God to atone for conceivable sinning. Job 1:5p, "It may be that my children have sinned, and cursed God in their hearts." Even when his wife, misleading, demanded that he, compliant, curse the LORD and die, Job 2:9, the man honored his marital commitments; he did not press a certificate of divorce into her hands and send her out of his house. Instead, through her he fathered ten more sons and daughters. In distinction from iniquitous fools, Job in wisdom averted his eyes from lustful intent. Job 31:1, "I have made a covenant with my eyes; how then shall I gaze at a virgin?" In wisdom, he refused allures of adultery.

> If my heart has been enticed toward a woman,
> and I have lain in wait at my neighbor's door,
> then let my wife grind for another,
> and let others bow down on her.
> Job 31:9

Simply, the man in recognition of his marital pledges and out of fear for the consequences of infidelity lived within mandated limits of marital faithfulness, therein finding freedom from lascivious temptations and freedom for connubial consummations.

2

Psalms 127–128 honor the uprightness of marital devotion; in the conviction that the LORD God builds every marital union, covenant men and covenant women conjugally bound find connubial fulfillment, raising God-given children in the fear of the LORD. Therefore the promissory,

> Behold,
> children are a heritage from the LORD,
> the fruit of the womb a reward.
> Like arrows in the hand of a warrior are the children of
> one's youth.
> Blessed is the man who fills his quiver with them!
> He shall not be put to shame when he speaks with his
> enemies in the gate.
> Psalm 127:35

Similarly, laudable praises for the Creator and Sustainer of sound unions transcend the ages.

Your wife will be like a fruitful vine within your house;
your children will be like olive shoots around your table.
Behold,
thus shall the man be blessed who fears the LORD.
Psalm 128:3–4

With hope, the praise-full Psalmist pressed Israelite men and women into male/female bonding, thereby upholding the masculine and feminine stabilizers that sustain the God-given strengths of marriage—whatever the paradigmatic power shifts of the times.

3

The Proverbs eye adulterous sinning, separating foolish adventurers[11] from the upright in heart. With the vital signs of wisdom,

. . . you will be delivered from the forbidden woman,
from the adulteress with her smooth words,
who forsakes the companion of her youth and forgets
the covenant of her God;
for her house sinks down to death,
and her paths to the departed;
none who go to her come back,
nor do they regain the paths of life.
Proverbs 2:16–19

The way of the honorable and the path of the righteous separate the wise from the sin-making fools; all who listen to the Word head into the good life, in every generation laden with the blessings of the LORD God.

In every generation the liberal-minded of the covenant communion walk the heady way of fools into eternal incineration.

For the lips of a forbidden woman drip honey,
and her speech is smoother than oil,
but in the end she is bitter as wormwood,
sharp as a two-edged sword.
Her feet go down to death;

11. Throughout Proverbs, the greater weight of condemnations falls on the men, abusers of masculinity content in ignorance.

her steps follow the path to Sheol;
she does not ponder the path of life;
her ways wander,
and she does not know it.
. . . . .
And now, O sons, listen to me,
and do not depart from the words of my mouth.
Keep your way far from her,
and do not go near the door of her house,
lest you give your honor to others and your years to the
merciless,
lest strangers take their fill of your strength,
and your labors go to the house of a foreigner,
and at the end of your life you groan,
when your flesh and body are consumed,
and you say, "How I hated discipline,
and my heart despised reproof!
I did not listen to the voice of my teachers or incline my
ear to my instructors.
I am at the brink of utter ruin in the assembled
congregation."
. . . . .
Drink water from your own cistern,
flowing water from your own well.
Should your springs be scattered abroad,
streams of water in the streets?
Let them be for yourself alone,
and not for strangers with you.
Let your fountain be blessed,
and rejoice in the wife of your youth,
a lovely deer, a graceful doe,
let her breasts fill you at all times with delight;
be intoxicated always in her love.
Why should you be intoxicated, my son, with a forbidden woman
and embrace the bosom of an adulteress?
Proverbs 5:3–20

Thus, all who maximally love wisdom find early the root stock
of fidelity that the LORD planted at the beginning of time and lasts
until the end of days. In contrast, fools miss the transparency of

wisdom; masochists, even as feminists, find the urges of the flesh superior to the blessed wisdom of the LORD and consider adultery a passing affection of no momentous worth, a conquest of sorts, perhaps.

Without mercy for adventurers, Solomon pressed home the negativity on the wrong side of the Seventh Commandment. Fools miss the transparency of this wisdom; masochists, even as feminists, find adultery a passing self-pleasuring. Hence . . .

> For the commandment is a lamp and the teaching a
> light,
> and the reproofs of discipline are the way of life,
> to preserve you from the evil woman,
> from the smooth tongue of the adulteress.
> Do not desire her beauty in your heart,
> and do not let her capture you with her eye lashes;
> for the price of a prostitute is only a loaf of bread,
> but a married woman hunts down a precious life.
> Can a man carry fire next to his chest and his clothes
> not be burned?
> Or can one walk on hot coals and his feet not be
> scorched?
> So is he who goes in to his neighbor's wife,
> none who touches her will go unpunished.
> Proverbs 6:23–29

Scriptures hold males to first accountability, Proverbs 6:32, "He who commits adultery lacks sense; he who does it destroys himself." In the glorious courts of the LORD, adulterers find they own lasting shame.

> He will get wounds and dishonor,
> and his disgrace will not be wiped away.
> Proverbs 6:33

The arrogance of an adulterer, momentarily to possess the body of a married woman, sees the door into damnation opening wide. With unrelenting acceleration, the wise author of the Proverbs uncovered the idiocy of sexual deviancy.

For at the window of my house I have looked out
through my lattice,
and I have seen among the simple,
I have perceived among the youths,
a young man lacking sense,
passing along the street near her corner,
taking the road to her house in the twilight of the
evening,
at the time of night and darkness.

. . . . .

And behold, the woman meets him,
dressed as a prostitute, wily of heart.
She is loud and wayward;
her feet do not stay at home;
now in the street, now in the market,
and at every corner she lies in wait.
She seizes him and kisses him,
and with bold face she says to him,
"I had to offer sacrifices,[12]
and today I have paid my vows;
so now I have come out to meet you,
to seek you eagerly, and I have found you.
I have spread my couch with coverings,
colored linens from Egyptian linen;
I have perfumed my bed with myrrh, aloes, and
cinnamon.
Come, let us take our fill of love till morning;
let us delight ourselves with love.
For my husband is not at home;
he has gone on a long journey;
he took a bag of money with him;
at full moon he will come home."

. . . . .

With much seductive speech she persuades him;
with her smooth talk she compels him.
All at once he follows her,
as an ox goes to the slaughter,

---

12. Sacrifices presented upon post-menstrual cleaning, Leviticus 15:19–28,
then verse 29, "And on the eighth she shall take two turtledoves or two pigeons
and bring them to the priest, to the entrance of the tent of meeting."

or as a stag is caught fast till an arrow pierces its liver;
as a bird rushes into a snare,
he does not know that it will cost him his life.
Proverbs 7:6–23

Throughout the Proverbs, the road signs punctuated messages of irreparable carnal damages deep into consciences; the LORD God will not have fouled relationships befouling covenant community. Yet, some commit to adultery, tawdry love of death preferable to love of life.

With the vigor of persistence and the stamina of persuasion, Wisdom speaks into open ears; she will have a hearing.

The woman Folly is loud;
she is seductive and knows nothing.
She sits at the door of her house;
she takes a seat on the highest places of the town,
calling to those who pass by,
who are going straight on their way,
"Whoever is simple, let him turn in here!"
And to him who lacks sense she says,
"Stolen water is sweet, and bread eaten in secret is
pleasant."
But he does not know that the dead are there,
that her guests are in the depths of Sheol.
Proverbs 9:13–18

And fools, no longer fools, listen intently, finding the way of life.

Repetitive condemnation to the contrary, masochism and feminism break whatever procrastination fools may discover. With obvious transparency, Wisdom commands the virtues of the forever one man/one woman directive, forcing problem-makers to face the irremovable facts of adultery. Therefore many evidences of exemplary marriages:

An excellent wife is the crown of her husband,
but she who brings shame (of adultery) is like rotten-
ness in his bones.
Proverbs 12:4

He who finds a wife finds a good thing[13] and obtains
favor from the LORD.
Proverbs 18:22

A foolish son is ruin to his father,
and a wife's quarreling is a continual dripping of rain.
House and wealth are inherited from fathers,
but a prudent wife is from the LORD.
Proverbs 19:13–14

It is better to live in a corner of the house top than in a
house shared with a quarrelsome wife.
Proverbs 21:9, 25:24[14]

It is better to live in a desert land than with a quarrelsome and fretful woman.
Proverbs 21:19

A continual dripping on a rainy day and a quarrelsome
wife are alike;
to restrain her is to restrain the wind or to grasp oil in
one's right hand.
Proverbs 27:15–16

As a rule of thumb, unless psychological disorders interfere,
husbands who neglect or manipulate wives for selfish ends find
that good wives turn crotchety and cantankerous.

After all admonitions to repulse adultery, Wisdom continu-
ally insists on a hearing by which to transform fools into living
members of the covenant community.

The mouth of forbidden women is a deep pit;
he with whom the LORD is angry will fall into it.
Proverbs 22:14

---

13. Without a feminine slight, this multivalent word upholds the worth of
righteous women, as in Proverbs 31:10–31.

14. Explaining the duplication: at Proverbs 25:1, the editor added another
collection of wisdom sayings.

For a prostitute is a deep pit;
an adulteress is a narrow well.
Proverbs 23:27

He who loves wisdom makes his father glad,
but a companion of prostitutes squanders his wealth.
Proverbs 29:3

This is the way of an adulteress:
she eats and wipes her mouth and says,
"I have done no wrong."
Proverbs 30:20

Do not give your strength to women,
your ways to those who destroy kings.
Proverbs 31:3

Wisdom—begun in the kinetic fear of the LORD—reforms men and women, sons and daughters to know marital fidelity. Ways into carnal intimacies lead to ultimate ruin. Only masculine men and feminine women know better. To exemplify serene Wisdom, the author presented the man and the woman of 31:10–31 in a marriage affirmation; he loved and respected and trusted her and she responded by upholding his name in the covenant community.

4

In Ecclesiastes 12:13–14, the entirety of life bloomed astonishingly in fearing God and keeping his commandments; for in the pending judgment, the satisfactions of many concubines, 2:8, brought only vanity and condemnation, whereas the prescriptive 9:9 saying vivified righteousness—"Enjoy life with the wife whom you love, all the days of your vain life that [the LORD] has given you under the sun, because that is your portion in life and your toil at which you toil under the sun." This always admirable wisdom enlightens the dreariness of all vanity with a measure of hope.

5

Of the 1,000 women to whom despotic Solomon had sexual access, one surprisingly stood apart. This rose of Sharon and lily of the valley represented Israel. At the beginning of his monarchy, David's son and successor truly loved the Israelite nation, the love for this one woman symbolic of his passions. Slowly, however, the tethering passions of the marital affections cooled, the allures the other wives and concubines' idolatry overpowering, 1 Kings 11:1–8, 33, and Solomon for all his wisdom turned into an inconsolable fool.

A Fourth Sum

In the revealed wisdom of Job, the Psalms, Proverbs, Ecclesiastes, and Solomon's Song, the biblical Author in meriting ways contrasted Wisdom and Folly, the one his gift and the other the human spirit in its natural environment. The live currents of wisdom coursed throughout the Old Testament manifestation of the Church, its felicity in every present the capacity to distinguish between the truth and the painfully abusive fallacies.

Goal-oriented Wisdom, emblematic of divine love, encompassed fidelity.[15]

THE END OF SEXUAL PERVERSITY

Upon the prophetic era, the LORD God halted the misogynistic idolatries that had repeatedly spiraled into predictable carnal perversities. As he prepared fornicating Israel for the Exile and as exiled Israelites settled in Mesopotamian lands, they in some sense recognized the divisive sins of fornication that had brought them into that ominous predicament.

---

15. Note: in Leviticus, Moses concentrated on incestuous sins and Solomon in Proverbs on adulterous sinning. The one reflected close confines associated with slavery, the other the permissiveness associated with idolatry. Changing paradigms changed fornicative possibilities.

1

Visionary Isaiah pointed out deep sins of fornication, perhaps less graphically than others, yet without minimizing carnal life choices. He likened Jerusalem to a slut, sluttish. Isaiah 1:21a, "How the faithful city has become a whore." He identified the city of the Lord with salacious worlds of dysfunctional sexuality, the whole of which lay defiled under its inhabitants, absent joys of life.

> The earth mourns and withers,
> the world languishes and withers;
> the highest people of the earth languish.
> The earth lies defiled under its inhabitants;
> for they have transgressed the laws,
> violated the statutes,
> broken the everlasting covenant.
> Isaiah 24:4–5

To complete his fascinating mandate, faithful Isaiah mocked idolatry, the acerbating axis of fornicative lusts.

> To whom then will you liken God,
> or what likeness compare with him?
> An idol! A craftsman casts it,
> and a gold smith overlays it with gold and casts for it
> silver chains.
> He who is too impoverished for an offering chooses
> wood that will not rot;
> he seeks out a skillful craftsman to set up an idol that
> will not move.
> Isaiah 40:18–20

With identical mockeries, Isaiah 41:7, 44:7, 48:5; etc., the LORD God denounced the lifestyles of idolatry; he willed marital wholeness and wholesomeness. The overbearing handmade gods of idolatry stimulated conventional lewdness, fornicative lasciviousness. In Jerusalem and Canaan, the prophet uncovered Israel's depths of whoring.

> But you, draw near,
> sons of the sorceress,

offspring of the adulterer and the loose woman.
Whom are you mocking?
Against whom do you open your mouth wide and stick
out your tongue?
Are you not children of transgression,
the offspring of deceit,
you who burn with lust among the oaks,
under every green tree,
who slaughter your children in the valleys,
under clefts of the rocks?
Among the smooth stones of the valley is your portion,
they, they are your lot;
to them you have poured out a drink offering,
you have brought a grain offering.
Shall I relent for these things?
On a high and lofty mountain you have set your bed,
and there you went up to offer sacrifice.
Behind the door and the doorpost you have set up your
memorial,
for, deserting me, you have uncovered your bed,
you have gone up to it,
you have made it wide;
and you have made a covenant for yourself with them,
you have loved their bed,
you have looked on nakedness.
Isaiah 57:3–8

King Hezekiah had removed idolatrous altars from the high places, Isaiah 36:7; 2 Kings 18:4, and yet Israel still plumbed hidden deeps for designs on a continuum of illicit sexual intimacies.

The LORD with due warning had prepared his people against the sexualized idolatries of Baalism. Deuteronomy 12:2–5, "You shall surely destroy all the places where the nations whom you shall dispossess served their gods, on the high mountains and on the hills and under every green tree. You shall tear down altars and dash in pieces their pillars and burn their Asherim with fire. You shall chop down the carved images of their gods and destroy their name out of that place. You shall not worship the LORD your God in that way. But you shall seek the place that the LORD your God will choose out of all your tribes to put his name and make his habitation there. There you shall go." All Israel's perverse searching and striving for banned sexual satisfactions was to come to an end in the looming exile on the day of the Lord. Israel's God intended to terminate every fornicative craving and make holiness prevail. Isaiah 17:7–8, "In that day man will look to his Maker and his eyes will look on the Holy One of Israel. He will not look to the altars, the work of his hands, and he will not look on what his own fingers have made, either the Asherim or the altars of incense." The geopolitical imminence of the day cast its alarming shadow over Jerusalem and Canaan, taking to heart thoroughgoing sanctification.

2

Jeremiah, explicitly, bared Israel's sexual hankerings and hungers, the covenant people idolatrously seduced to seek carnal gratifications beyond pagan penchants and preferences.

> A voice on the bare heights is heard,
> the weeping and pleading of Israel's sons because they
> have perverted their way;
> they have forgotten the LORD their God.
> "Return, O faithless sons;
> I will heal your faithlessness."
> "Behold, we come to you,
> for you are the LORD our God.
> Truly, the hills are a delusion,
> the orgies on the mountains.
> Truly in the LORD our God is the salvation of Israel."
> Jeremiah 3:21–23

Yet, whatever the remorse and the entreaty, Israel had ossified on the edge of existence. Therefore the LORD God called out and specified delusional gratifications.

> "If you return, O Israel,"
> declares the LORD,
> "to me you should return.
> If you remove your detestable things from my presence,

and do not waver,
and if you swear, 'As the LORD lives,'
in truth, in justice, and in righteousness,
then nations shall bless themselves in him,
and in him shall they glory."
For thus says the LORD to the men of Judah and
Jerusalem:
"Break up your fallow ground,
and sow not among thorns.
Circumcise yourselves to the LORD,
remove the foreskins of your hearts,
O men of Judah and inhabitants of Jerusalem;
lest my wrath go forth like fire,
and burn with none to quench it,
because of the evil of your deeds."
Jeremiah 4:1–4

The reference to circumcision called the people to procreative faithfulness, as the LORD God once summoned Abraham to marital integrity, Genesis 17:10, but Israel on common ground with strangers to grace refused to hear and obey.

For my people are foolish;
they know me not;
they are stupid children;
they have no understanding.
They are wise—in doing evil!
but how to do good they know not.
Jeremiah 4:22

Preferences for epoch-making fornicative envies moved the Church, with the result that they, willfully blind, remained irrevocably mired in carnal sinning.

And you, O desolate one,
what do you mean that you dress in scarlet,
that you adorn yourself with ornaments of gold,
that you enlarge your eyes with paint?
In vain you beautify yourself.
Your lovers despise you;
they seek your life.
Jeremiah 4:30

Locked away in reprobation, Israel lacked the lively passions of repentance to reenter faithfulness, even for mitigating whore activities. The prophet speaking . . .

> O LORD, do not your eyes look for truth?
> You have struck them down,
> but they felt no anguish;
> you have consumed them,
> but they refused to take correction.
> They have made their faces harder than rock;
> they have refused to repent.
> Jeremiah 5:3

The people bound in the day of the Lord for exile toughened themselves against Jeremiah's divine appeal, the pleasures of the flesh worth exploiting, they indifferent to the dark tomorrows for the rising generations. Sharply, the unshakable prophet unfolded the future chain of information in the present. The LORD speaking . . .

> How can I pardon you?
> Your children have forsaken me and have sworn by
> those who are no gods.
> When I fed them to the full,
> they committed adultery and trooped to the houses of
> whores.
> They were well-fed, lusty stallions,
> each neighing for his neighbor's wife.
> Jeremiah 5:7–9

Whatever barrages of forewarnings, Judah and Jerusalem, even as Nebuchadnezzar's military hordes loomed on the evolving horizon, refused the only acceptable way of the LORD.

> Flee for safety, O people of Benjamin,
> from the midst of Jerusalem!
> Blow the trumpet[16] in Tekoa,
> and raise a signal on Beth-haccherem,
> for disaster looms out of the north,
> and great destruction.
> Jeremiah 6:1

16. Israel heard the Numbers 10:9 trumpet alarm echoing throughout the Church.

Still, the LORD God with the patience of longsuffering willed remorse and repentance. So Jeremiah 7:5–7. "For if you truly amend your ways and your deeds, if you truly execute justice one with another, if you do not oppress the sojourner, the fatherless, or the widow, or shed innocent blood in this place, and if you do not go out after other gods to your own harm, then I will let you dwell in this place, in the land that I gave of old to your fathers forever." However, the unrestrained tumults of Baalism as of old pleased Israel more. Jeremiah 7:30–32, "For the sons of Judah have done evil in my sight, declares the LORD. They have set their detestable things in the house that is called by my name to defile it. And they have built the high places of Topheth, which is in the Valley of the Son of Hinnom, to burn their sons and their daughters in the fire, which I did not command, nor did it come into my mind. Therefore, behold, the days are coming, declares the LORD, when it will no more be called Topheth, or the Valley of the Son of Hinnom, but the Valley of Slaughter; for they shall bury in Topheth, because there is no room elsewhere." Such the abhorrent massacres at Nebuchadnezzar's invasion.

In Lamentations 1:19, Jeremiah raised Jerusalem's lament of despair. Too late the people expressed regrets.

> I called to my lovers,
> but they deceived me;
> my priests and elders perished in the city,
> while they sought food to revive their strength.

Prophetic Jeremiah throughout the totality of his inspired foresights and compelling forecasts called out to a people that blocked the voice of the LORD.

3

Ezekiel ministered among the Israelite captives settling in Babylonian lands. To extinguish any hope among the exiles, he prophesied the fall of Jerusalem. Ezekiel 6:1–4, "The word of the LORD came to me, 'Son of man, set your face toward the mountains of Israel, and prophesy against them, and say, You mountains of Israel, hear the word of the LORD GOD! Thus says the LORD GOD to the mountains and the hills, to the ravines and the valleys: Behold, I, even I, will bring a sword upon you, and I will destroy your high places. Your altars shall become desolate, and your incense altars shall be broken, and I will cast down your slain before your idols.'" Amidst these onerous denunciations and censures, the LORD remembered the Exodus as courtship and marital union, 16:1–14. Then . . .

> But you trusted in your beauty and played the whore because of your renown and lavished your whorings on any passerby; your beauty became his. You took some of your garments and made for yourself colorful shrines, and on them played the whore. The like has never been, nor ever shall be. You also took your beautiful jewels of my gold and of my silver, which I had given you, and made for yourself images of men, and with them played the whore. Ezekiel 16:15–22

In this fatal deviancy, the prophet made comparisons, Judah to the Philistines, Judah to Northern Israel, and Judah once more to Northern Israel. Ezekiel 16:27, ". . . I stretched out my hand against you and diminished your allotted portion and delivered you to the greed of your enemies, the daughters of the Philistines, who were ashamed of your lewd behavior." Ezekiel 16:47, "Not only did you walk in their ways and do according to their abominations; within a very little time you were more corrupt than they in all your ways." Ezekiel 16:51, "Samaria has not committed half your sins. You have more abominations than they, and have made your sisters appear righteous by all the abominations that you have committed."

On and on, Ezekiel displayed Israel's infidelities, a prostitute paying for public adulteries. Ezekiel 16:35–37, "Therefore, O prostitute, hear the word of the LORD. Thus says the LORD GOD, Because your lust was poured out and your nakedness uncovered in your whorings with your lovers, and with all your abominable idols, and because of the blood of your children that you gave to them, therefore, behold, I will gather all your lovers with whom you took pleasure, all those you loved and all those you hated. I will gather them against you from every side and will uncover your nakedness to them, that they may see all your nakedness." Jeremiah on and on exposed Israel's adulteries and fornications, the whole concentrated in 23:1–49, condemning Oholah and Oholibah, the first representing Northern Israel, the second Judah. Oholibah exceeded Oholah in carnal perversities, which Ezekiel depicted with unadulterated starkness.

Consequently, Ezekiel 16:43, "Because you have not remembered the days of your youth, but have enraged me with all these [infidelities], therefore, behold, I have returned your deeds upon your head, declares the LORD GOD. Have you not committed lewdness in addition to all your abominations?" Still, the LORD revealed his faithfulness to the new covenant bond to accomplish Genesis 3:14–15, the Serpent the loser in every generation. Ezekiel 16:59–60, "For thus says the LORD GOD: I will deal with you as you have done, you who despised the oath in breaking the covenant, yet I will remember my covenant with you in the days of youth, and I will establish for you an everlasting covenant." Thus, as the prophetic age drew to a close, the LORD God revealed the hope in the Adam-and-Eve marriage, the one that procreates sons and daughters in the believing way.

Sharper than Isaiah, Hosea, and Jeremiah, Ezekiel in the 23rd chapter described the horrors of fornication, the end of which the Nebuchadnezzar invasion; as the captive Israelites walked to Mesopotamia, interests in fornication fell by the wayside. Ezekiel 23:46–49, "For thus says the LORD GOD, 'Bring up a vast host against them, and make them an object of terror and a plunder. And the host shall stone them and cut them down with their swords. They shall kill their sons and their daughters, and burn up their houses. Thus will I put an end to lewdness in the land, that all women may take warning and not commit lewdness as you have done. And they shall return your lewdness upon you, and you shall bear the penalty for your sinful idolatry, and you shall know that I am the LORD GOD." For all the abominable fornications of the

Church, the LORD willed otherwise—to have the last imperishable word.

4

Hosea, at the LORD's command, married Gomer, whose prostitution symbolized Israel's unfaithfulness, 1:2–3. Therefore, to Israel's sons and daughters, children of infidelity,

> Plead with your mother, plead
> —for she is not my wife, and I am not her husband—
> that she put away her whoring from her face,
> and her adultery from between her breasts;
> lest I strip her naked and make her as in the day she was
> born,
> and make her like a wilderness,
> and make her like a parched land,
> and kill her with thirst.
> Upon her children also I will have no mercy,
> because they are children of whoredom.
> For their mother has played the whore;
> she who conceived them has acted shamefully.
> For she said, "I will go after my lovers,
> who gave me my bread and my water,
> my wool and my flax, my oil and my drink."
> Hosea 2:2–5

Merciless in exposing Israel's adaptations to the whoring Baal-world, the Lord revealed his the day of judgment.

> Now I will uncover her lewdness in the sight of her
> lovers,
> and no one shall rescue her out of my hand.
> And I will put an end to all her mirth,
> her feasts, her new moons, her Sabbaths,
> and all her appointed feasts.
> And I will lay waste her vines and her fig trees,
> of which she said,
> "These are my wages,
> which my lovers have given me."

I will make them a forest,
and the beasts of the field shall devour them.
And I will punish her for the feast days of the Baals
when she burned offerings to them and adorned herself
with her ring and jewelry
and went after her lovers and forgot me,
declares the LORD.

Hosea 2:10–13

Yet in the sovereignty of grace, the LORD God revealed divine initiative in leading Israel into repentance.

Therefore, behold, I will allure her,
and bring her into the wilderness,
and speak tenderly to her.
And there I will give her her vineyards and make the
Valley of Achor a door of hope.
And there she shall answer as in the days of her youth,
as at the time when she came out of the land of Egypt.

Hosea 2:14–15

The LORD promised sanctification. Hosea 2:16–20, "And in that day, declares the LORD, you will call me 'My Husband,' and no longer will you call me, 'My Baal.' For I will remove the names of the Baals from her mouth, and they shall be remembered by name no more. . . . And I will betroth you to me forever. I will betroth you to me in righteousness and in justice, in steadfast love and in mercy. I will betroth you to me in faithfulness. And you shall know the LORD."

Yet, the LORD, to strengthen the imagery of unfaithfulness, summoned Hosea to marry an adulteress, 3:1–5. None however willed to acknowledge the symbolism and seek the way of reformation, a fact of Ephraim's continual whoring.

Ephraim is joined to idols,
leave him alone.
When their drink is gone,
they give themselves to whoring;
their rulers dearly love shame.

A wind has wrapped them in its wings,
and they shall be ashamed because of their sacrifices.
Hosea 4:17–19

At the end of his ministry, with an eye on the day of the Lord, the prophet nevertheless in hope appealed to his people.

Whoever is wise, let him understand these things;
whoever is discerning, let him know them;
for the ways of the LORD are right,
and the upright walk in them,
but transgressors stumble in them.
Hosea 14:9

5

Throughout the other prophets, fornicative sinning gained less attention; each condemned idolatry and the social evils that evolved from serving man-made gods—demeaning the poor, widows, orphans, and strangers; by taking advantage of the helpless, the idolaters found a life of ease. Amos pointed to an incestuous case, 2:7, satisfying carnal urges about pagan altars, 2:8, and wives selling respective bodies for food, 7:17. Micah scorned the fees of prostitution, 1:7, Zechariah predicted the rape of wives by enemy armies, and Malachi sentenced infidelity, 2:15, as well as the hatred that caused divorce, 2:16. On the whole, Israel blended in with the surrounding nations, seeking the comforts of assimilation, the ending to which the LORD God prophesied for the disparaged day of reckoning.

6

The day of the Lord came, first for the Ten Tribes, then for Judah. The LORD God willed that all social pollutions, among which the fornicative transgressions, stop, and his people heart-understand the necessity also of marital holiness for the Faith.

The end of fornication came, in 722 BC for Northern-Israel's survivors of Assyrian massacres and in 587 BC for Judean survivors of Babylonian massacres; they walked in long rows to face exile for many decades.

And this occurred because the people of Israel had sinned against the LORD their God, who had brought them up out of the land of Egypt from under the hand of Pharaoh king of Egypt, and had feared other gods and walked in the customs of the nations whom the LORD drove out before the people of Israel, and in the customs that the kings of Israel had practiced. And the people of Israel did secretly against the LORD their God things that were not right. They built for themselves high places in all their towns from watchtower to fortified city. They set up for themselves pillars and Asherim on every high hill and under every green tree, and there they made offerings on all the high places, as the nations did whom the LORD carried away before them. And they did wicked things, provoking the LORD to anger, and they served idols, of which the LORD to them, "You shall not do this." Yet the LORD warned Israel and Judah by every prophet and every seer, saying, 'Turn from your evil ways and keep my commandments and my statutes in accordance with all the Law that I commanded your fathers, and that I sent to you by my servants the prophets."

But they would not listen, but were stubborn, as their fathers had been, who did not believe in the LORD their God. They despised his statutes and his covenant that he made with their fathers and the warnings that he gave them. They went after false gods and became false, and they followed the nations that were around them, concerning whom the LORD had commanded them that they should not do like them. And they abandoned all the commandments of the LORD their God, and made for themselves metal images of two calves; and they made an Asherah and worshiped all the host of heaven and served Baal. And they burned their sons and their daughters as offerings and used divination and omen and sold themselves to do evil in the sight of the LORD, provoking him to anger. Therefore the LORD was very angry with Israel and removed them out of his sight. None was left but the tribe of Judah only.

Judah also did not keep the commandments of the LORD their God, but walked in the customs that Israel had introduced. And the LORD rejected all the descendants of Israel and afflicted them and gave them into the hand of plunderers, until he had cast them out of his sight. Second Kings 17:7–18

A Fifth Sum

At long last, the LORD God, losing patience with his idolatrous and fornicative people, walked them off into exile, first the Assyrian and then the Babylonian. In the walking away from Canaan and in the strangeness of Mesopotamian lands, that covenant generation, maximally sunk in illusions, *saw* the fool's paradise they had latterly built.

THE HOPE OF HUMAN SEXUALITY

Out of prophetic depths ascended the energetic marriage analogy, the LORD God the faithful Husband, the Church the Bride, however faithless the Israelite men and women; the divine faithfulness founded the hope inspired by the Adam-Eve union—one man and one woman united for life.

1

In the eighth-century BC, surprising, Isaiah asserted the analogical husband-wife bond between the LORD God and Israel, the purpose of which to reveal the awesome Husband's faithfulness and to summon the Bride to fidelity.

"Fear not,
for you will not be ashamed;
be not confounded,

for you will not be disgraced;
for you will forget the shame of your youth,
and the reproach of your widowhood you will remember no more.
For your Maker is your husband,
the LORD of hosts is his name;
and the Holy One of Israel is your Redeemer,
the God of the whole earth he is called.
For the LORD has called you like a wife deserted and
grieved in spirit,
like a wife of youth when she is cast off,
says your God.
For a brief moment I deserted you,
but with great compassion I will gather you.
In overflowing anger for a moment I hid my face from
you,
but with everlasting love I will have compassion on
you,"
says the LORD, your Redeemer.
Isaiah 54:4–8

I will greatly rejoice in the LORD;
my soul shall exult in my God,
for he has clothed me with the garments of salvation,
as a bridegroom decks himself like a priest with a beautiful headdress,
and as a bride adorns herself with her jewels.
Isaiah 61:10

The grace of the LORD God's bond with Israel consisted in
the fact that the Husband recreated the men and the women who
represented his Spouse. The groundbreaking prophet exegeted this
marital union . . .

You shall no more be termed Forsaken,
and your land shall no more be termed Desolate,
but you shall be called My Delight Is in Her,
and your land Married,
for the LORD delights in you,
and your land shall be married.
For as a young man marries a young woman,

so shall your sons marry you,
and as the bridegroom rejoices over the bride,
so shall your God rejoice over you.
Isaiah 62:4–5

Out of breathtaking God-given resources of prophecy, this marital union created hope for the eternally acceptable experience of human sexuality. If the LORD is faithful, so—by grace—can the men and the women of the Church.

2

Hosea, also of the eighth-century BC, had to marry a prostitute, a wife of whoredom, Gomer, to display the faithfulness of the LORD God, She, in her unfaithfulness, representative of the Old Testament Church, embodied the men and the women who easily resorted to idolatry with its carnal pleasures. Then Hosea prophesied, to end Israel's repetitive whoring,

She shall pursue her lovers but not overtake them,
and she shall seek them,
but shall not find them.
Then she shall say,
"I will go and return to my first husband,
for it was better for me then than now."
Hosea 2:7

In the day-of-the-Lord leading into the Exile, Hosea prophetically declared the LORD's faithfulness, telling the men and the women of the Church that only the Adam-and-Eve standard sufficed to express human sexuality. Hopefully, the prophet reached ahead.

3

Jeremiah began the God–Israel bond that the Exodus graphically illustrated, the LORD speaking.

> I remember the devotion of your youth,
> your love as a bride,
> how you followed me in the wilderness,
> in a land not sown.
> Israel was holy to the LORD,
> the firstfruits of his harvest.
> All who ate of it incurred guilt,
> disaster came upon them,
> declares the LORD.
> Jeremiah 2:2–3

Analogically, with new-wed passion, the LORD God *owned* Israel, as a new husband his bride, promising the forever continuity in unity.

Despite Israel's repetitive adulteries, the LORD nevertheless recreated a renewed bond. Jeremiah 31:32–33, "Behold, the days are coming, declares the LORD, when I will make a new covenant with the house of Israel and the house of Judah, not like the covenant that I made with their fathers on the day I took them by the hand to bring them out of the land of Egypt, my covenant that they broke, though I was their husband, declares the LORD." At the same time, at the awe-inspiring construction of the new covenant, Israel's husband separated the elect from the reprobate in order to own a pure bride, which escalated the hope embodied in every God-fearing marital union.

4

Ezekiel, more graphic then Jeremiah, referred to the Exodus as the beginning of the unique God-Israel marriage, he the Maker of her femininity.

> When I passed by you again and saw you, behold, you were at the age of love, and I spread the corner of my garment over you and covered your nakedness; I made my vow to you and entered into a covenant with you, declares the LORD GOD, and you became mine. Then I bathed you and anointed you with oil. I clothed you also with embroidered cloth and shod you with fine leather. I

wrapped you in fine linen and covered you with silk. And
I adorned you with ornaments and put bracelets on your
wrists and a chain on your neck. And I put a ring on your
nose and earrings in your ears and a beautiful crown on
your head. Thus you were adorned with gold and silver
and embroidered cloth. You also ate fine flour and honey
and oil. You grew exceedingly beautiful and advanced to
royalty. And your renown went forth among the nations
because of your beauty, for it was perfect through the
splendor that I had bestowed on you, declares the LORD.
Ezekiel 16:5–14

A Sixth Sum

In accord with the Old Testament's history of the Recreation, believers submitted to the recreation of masculinity and femininity,
the men never daring masochism and the women never wielding
feminism. Others segregated masculinity from femininity and
femininity from masculinity by falling into ideological abstrac-
tions, men spiraling down into masochists and women into feminists. Each stand-alone gender reduced men into anti-masculine
manhood, objectifying womanhood, and degraded women into
anti-feminine womanhood, objectifying manhood, both processes
of self-identification stimulating unpredictable agonies.

Exile into Mesopotamian lands impoverished the people;
they struggled for mere survival. In this dilemma, self-expression
in human sexuality failed. As the fictional gods they had whole-
heartedly worshiped faded away, impotent, the exiles, on the edge
of existence, strove for subsistence rather than entertain carnal
irregularities of the past. And in the post-exilic centuries, the
people listened to Ezra and Nehemiah, Haggai and Zechariah to
concentrate on lasting holiness primarily by renouncing affinity
for intermarriages, the then current transition into idolatry.

. . . . .

Faithfully, from prophetic heights, the LORD God summoned forth the marriage analogy, eternalizing hope for the

Church to break forth in the second dispensation, regenerating the heart intimacies that transcended the ages, because he had made them male and female.

Reformation Of Intimate Designs

AFTER MILLENNIA OF PAGAN masochism and now after multi-decades of troubling, indeed, domineering feminism—women coopting authoritarianism, men failing at headship, leadership[1]—the LORD God, Jesus, in every day reveals timely New Testament truths regarding the male/female stabilizers.

Delving into and reflecting on these New Testament verities stabilizing male/female submission to sexual designs moves in a singular tradition intended for all times and places. For this self-examination—congregationally, maritally and individually—Jesus conformed his marital teaching to the commandments and the tradition that he, the LORD God created.[2] For the regulation, foundation, and confirmation of marriage throughout the coming days, years, decades, and possibly centuries:

1. One, Promise Keepers, a 1990 Bill McCartney creation for men to reclaim masculinity in marital fidelity.

Two, Christian Nationalism, a Trumpian-infused political movement to promote white supremacy instilling racism, Anti-Semitism, anti-transgenderism, anti-homosexualism, to safeguard Caucasian purity. This far-right, neo-Nazi, ugly truth revives Third-Reich machismo.

Three, various right-wing movements as the Proud Boys seeking political traction for large empowerment.

2. Pp. 12–13 above.

consider the Incarnation the betrothal,
consider the Crucifixion the bride's price,
and consider the eschatological consummation the wedding feast.

In this intriguing arrangement, the Hebrew marriage pattern emerges, analogically displaying the Christ/Church bond.[3]

THE BETROTHAL OF CHRIST AND CHURCH

In the profundity of this awing mystery, God the Father, God the Son, and God the Spirit in the fullness of time created the Incarnation, the Three as One uniting God the Son with the humanity of a man, which occurred at Jesus' conception.

1

Hence, the Incarnation accounts of Matthew, Luke, John,[4] and Paul, whatever dissimilarities in presentation, reveal the exulting union of Jesus' divinity and humanity.

> Now the birth of Jesus Christ took place in this way. When his mother Mary had been betrothed to Joseph, before they came together she was found to be with child from the Holy Spirit. And her husband Joseph, being a just man and unwilling to put her to shame, resolved to divorce her quietly. But as he considered these things, behold, and angel of the Lord appeared to him in a dream, saying, "Joseph, son of David, do not fear to take Mary as your wife, for that which is conceived in her is from the Holy Spirit. She will bear a son, and you shall call his name Jesus, for he will save his people from their sins." All this took place to fulfill what the LORD had spoken by the prophet,

---

3. This captivating analogy breaks down in two ways: no authority figure emerges entrusted with the bride's price and no dowry appears in the Bride's hands.

4. The two-three witnesses necessary for juridical credibility, Deuteronomy 19:15–21.

"Behold, the virgin shall conceive and bear a son,
and they shall call his name Immanuel"[5]

(which means, God with us). When Joseph woke
from sleep, he did as the angel of the Lord commanded
him; he took his wife, but knew her not until she had
given birth to a son. And he called his name Jesus. Matthew 1:18–25

. . . . .

In the sixth month (of Elizabeth's pregnancy) the angel
Gabriel was sent from God to a city of Galilee named
Nazareth, to a virgin betrothed to a man whose name
was Joseph, of the house of David. And the virgin's name
was Mary. And he came to her and said, "Greetings, O
favored one, the Lord is with you!" But she was greatly
troubled at the saying, and tried to discern what sort of
greeting this might be. And the angel said to her, "Do not
be afraid, Mary, for you have found favor with God. And
behold, you will conceive in your womb and bear a son,
and you shall call his name Jesus. He will be great and
will be called the Son of the Most High. And the Lord
God will give him the throne of his father David, and
he will reign over the house of Jacob forever, and of his
kingdom there will be no end."

And Mary said to the angel, "How will this be, since
I am a virgin?"

And the angel answered her, "The Holy Spirit will
come upon you, and the power of the Most High will
overshadow you; therefore the child to be born will be
called holy—the Son of God. And behold, your relative
Elizabeth in her old age has also conceived a son, and
this is the sixth month with her who was called barren.
For nothing will be impossible with God." And Mary
said, "Behold, I am the servant of the Lord; let it be to me
according to your word." And the angel departed from
her. Luke 1:26–38

Matthew and Luke revealed the trinitarian secrecy of
the Incarnation and Mary's response (in a sense) represented
Israel's acceptance of the betrothal. Considering Matthew's

5. Isaiah 7:14.

husband-wife-divorce language, betrothal constituted a conjugal marriage ceremony, its consummation at a later date.

In the Christ/Church betrothal, the bride's price consisted of the promise of life inherent in the Crucifixion/Resurrection; nothing appears in the Scriptures that suggests that the Son of God gave the bride's price to God the Father for safekeeping. At the Crucifixion/Resurrection actuality, he entrusted the whole of the bride's price to the Church directly. And the Bride prepares herself throughout the second dispensation, sanctifying, cleansing herself of fornicative idolatries or idolatrous fornications. Because this marriage is of grace, the Church enters the consummation empty-handed, only her heart overflowing with gratitude.

Now, John and Paul's respective interpretations of the Incarnation:

> And the Word became flesh and dwelt among us, and we have seen his glory, glory as of the only Son from the Father, full of grace and truth. John 1:14

> . . . though he was in the form of God, did not count equality with God a thing to be grasped, but made himself nothing, taking the form of a servant, being born in the likeness of men. And being found in human form, he humbled himself by becoming obedient to the point of death, even death on a cross.[6] Philippians 2:6–8

These apostles asserted the bond between Jesus' divinity and humanity. His divinity, omnipresent, filled heaven and earth, thus his humanity too, yet through the creativity of God the Father and God the Spirit, they in Jesus forever united his divinity to his humanity, or his humanity to his divinity. By taking this humanity in the always amazing and impenetrable Incarnation, Jesus in effect bonded himself eternally to the humanity of the Church, she in her humanity united with him.

---

6. Other Pauline incarnational interpretations: Romans 1:2–3, 8:3b–4; 2 Corinthians 8:9; Galatians 4:4; Ephesians 4:8–10. Note also, Hebrews 2:14–16, 10:5–7; 1 Peter 1:20–21.

In his ministry, Jesus drew the consequences of the betrothal, the Church his Bride forever. For the men and women of the Bride, this longevity grounded marriage, confirming in the holiness of nuptials the prohibitions against fornicative acts and divorce. First, from Matthew.

> And Pharisees came up to him and tested him by asking, "Is it lawful to divorce one's wife for any cause?" He answered, "Have you not read that he who created them from the beginning made them male and female, and said, 'Therefore a man shall leave his father and his mother and hold fast to his wife, and the two shall become one flesh?' So they are no longer two but one flesh. What therefore God has joined together, let not man separate." They said to him, "Why then did Moses command one to give a certificate of divorce and to send her away?" He said to them, "Because of your hardness of heart Moses allowed you to divorce your wives, but from the beginning it was not so. And I say to you: whoever divorces his wife, except for sexual immorality, and marries another, commits adultery." Matthew 19:2–9

Similarly, from Mark: whomever Jesus bonds in marriage, he commits the man and the woman to marital longevity with an affinity for fidelity, for as long as both shall live. Divorce offers no excuse, either to the man or the woman to remarry.

> And Pharisees came up and in order to test him asked, "Is it lawful for a man to divorce his wife?" He answered them, "What did Moses command you?" They said, "Moses allowed a man to write a certificate of divorce and to send her away." And Jesus said to them, "Because of your hardness of heart he wrote you this commandment. But from the beginning of creation, 'God made them male and female.' Therefore a man shall leave his father and mother and hold fast to his wife, and the two shall become one flesh.' So they are no longer two but

one. What therefore God has joined together, let not man separate."[7]

And in the house the disciples asked him again about this matter. And he said to them, "Whoever divorces his wife and marries another commits adultery against her, and if she divorces her husband and marries another, she commits adultery." Mark 10:2–12

According to Matthew, 19:10–12, the disciples caught the tension between the radicality of Jesus' teaching and the demoralization of divorce. "The disciples said to him, 'If such is the case of a man with his wife, it is better not to marry.'" But he said to them. "Not everyone can receive this saying, but only those to whom it is given. For there are eunuchs who have been so from birth, and there are eunuchs who have been made eunuchs by men, and there are eunuchs who have made themselves eunuchs for the sake of the kingdom of heaven. Let the one who is able to receive this receive it." Divorce then makes men and women *eunuchs*, for all the condemnation reserved for adultery falls on those who remarry.

. . . . .

Luke also, in an age and among people in which dissolution of nuptials happened, stressed Jesus' proscription on remarriage upon divorce. Luke 16:18, "Everyone who divorces his wife and marries another commits adultery, and he who marries a woman divorced from her husband commits adultery." In his Bride and for the people who comprised her, Jesus revealed the forever of wedlock, no adulterous permissiveness granted.

Further, to preserve the holiness of marriage in his Bride, Jesus commanded far ranging and deep reaching injunctions.

You have heard that is was said, "You shall not commit adultery." But I say to you that everyone who looks at a woman with lustful intent has already committed adultery with her in his heart. If your right eye causes you to sin, tear it out and throw it away. For it is better that you

---

7. Only adultery, or another fornicative act, lays grounds for divorce. Divorce's radicality situates two people in loneliness and in temptation to remarry. First Corinthians 7:10–11.

lose one of your members than that your whole body be thrown into hell. And if your right hand causes you to sin, cut it off and throw it away. For it is better that you lose one of your members than that your whole body go into hell.

It was also said, "Whoever divorces his wife, let him give her a certificate of divorce." But I say to you that everyone who divorces his wife, except on the ground of sexual immorality, makes her commit adultery, and whoever marries a divorced woman commits adultery." Matthew 5:27–32

All whom the Lord Jesus marvelously bonds in marriage remain so, no excuses for divorce except sexual immorality. And no man, and no woman, dares to appear before the Judge of all the earth, Jesus, married to two (or more through serial monogamy) spouses simultaneously. Divorce never eradicates the fact of the first marriage, not while both husband and wife live.

Sadducees, who took the seriousness of marriage casually, made a petty attempt to mock the Lord Jesus' standard for marital longevity.

The same day (when Jesus had distinguished between paying taxes to Caesar and giving him due praise) Sadducees came to him, who say that there is no resurrection, and they asked him a question, saying, "Teacher, Moses said, 'If a man dies having no children, his brother must marry the widow and raise up children for his brother.' Now there were seven brothers among us. The first married and died, and having no children left his wife to his brother. So too the second and third, down to the seventh. After them all, the woman died. In the resurrection, therefore, of the seven, whose wife will she be? For they all had her.[8]

But Jesus answered them. "You are wrong, because you know neither the scriptures nor the power of God. For in the resurrection they neither marry nor are given

8. 1) Levirate marriage applied only to the first son, Deuteronomy 25:5–10.
2) The hyperbole indicated an attempt to embarrass Jesus, God, publicly, proof of reprobation.

in marriage, but are like angels in heaven. And as for the resurrection of the dead, have you not read what was said to you by God: "I am the God of Abraham, and the God of Isaac, and the God of Jacob? He is not God of the dead, but of the living."[9] And when the crowd heard it, they were astonished at his teaching. Matthew 22:23–33

And Jesus said to [those Sadducees], "The sons of this age marry and are given in marriage, but those who are considered worthy to attain to that age and to the resurrection from the dead neither marry nor are given in marriage, for they cannot die anymore, because they are equal to angels and are sons of God, being sons of the resurrection. But that the dead are raised, even Moses showed, in the passage about the bush, where he called the Lord the God of Abraham and the God of Isaac and the God of Jacob.[10] Now he is not the God of the dead, but of the living, for all live to him." Luke 20:34–38

In his ministry, Jesus condemned all carnal immoralities that he had registered throughout Old Testament history, damning every abuse of human sexuality.

3

Over three years of simple and direct ministry, the Lord and Savior by way of attention-getting parables taught the men and women of his Bride to highly respect the marital institution.

The kingdom of heaven may be compared to a king who gave a wedding feast for his son, and sent his servants to call those who were invited to the wedding feast, but they would not come. Again he sent other servants, saying, "Tell those who are invited, See, I have prepared my dinner, my oxen and my fat calves have been slaughtered, and everything is ready. Come to the wedding feast." But

9. Exodus 6:3a, "I appeared to Abraham, to Isaac, and to Jacob, as God Almighty."

10. Exodus 3:15a/Acts 3:13a, "The God of Abraham, the God of Isaac, and the God of Jacob, the God of our fathers, glorified his servant Jesus."

they paid no attention and went off, one to his farm, another to his business, while the rest seized his servants, treated them shamefully, and killed them. The king was angry, and he sent his troops and destroyed those murderers and burned their city. Then he said to his servants, "The wedding feast is ready, but those invited were not worthy. Go therefore to the main roads and invite to the wedding feast as many as you find." And those servants went out into roads and gathered all whom they found, both bad and good. So the wedding hall was filled with guests. Matthew 22:1–10

Now he told a parable to those who were invited, when he noticed how they chose the places of honor, saying to them, "When you are invited by someone to a wedding feast, do not sit down in a place of honor, lest someone more distinguished than you be invited by him, and he who invited you both will come and say to you, 'Give your place to this person,' and then you will begin with shame to take the lowest place. But when you are invited, go and sit in the lowest place, so that when your host comes he may say to you, 'Friend, move up higher.' Then you will be honored in the presence of all who sit at table with you. For everyone who exalts himself will be humbled, and he who humbles himself will be exalted." Luke 14:7–11

And then there is John 2:1–11, the account of Jesus' honored presence at a wedding in Cana during which he turned water into a superb wine.

A Seventh Sum

From the day of the Incarnation that began at his conception, the binding of his divinity and humanity, Jesus prepared the Church for the nuptial ceremony, the eschatological wedding feast. As Jesus called his Bride to holiness and she prepares herself for the consummation, then the men and the women who constitute her have to conform every marriage affirmation to the holiness of his divinity.

THE SUBMISSION OF THE BRIDE'S PRICE

Jesus chose to present his bride's price after the betrothal, the astonishing sacrifice of his humanity on Golgotha's Cross. The guarantee for this assurance he secured with numerous pertinent Old Testament prophecies and with Gospel pledges throughout his ministry. This bride's price he gave directly to the Church, her life's sustenance through the generations and ages leading into the wedding feast.

1

First, a selection of Old Testament prophecies, remarkable assurances of the LORD God's faithfulness:

Because you (the Serpent) have done this,
cursed are you above all lifestock and above all beasts of
the field;
on your belly you shall go,
and dust you shall eat all the days of your life.
I (the LORD) will put enmity between you and the
woman,
and between your offspring and her offspring;
he shall bruise your head,
and you shall bruise his heel.
Genesis 3:14–15

And your house and your kingdom shall be made sure
forever before me.
Your throne shall be established forever.
2 Samuel 7:16; 1 Chronicles 17:13–14

The LORD has sworn and will not change his mind,
"You are a priest forever after the order of Melchizedek."
Psalm 110:4; Hebrews 7:1–25

> Behold, my servant shall act wisely;
> he shall be high and lifted up,
> and shall be exalted.
> As many were astonished at you
> —his appearance was so marred,
> beyond human semblance,
> and his form beyond that of the children of mankind—
> so shall he [startle] many nations;
> kings shall shut their mouths because of him;
> for that which has not been told them they see,
> and that which they have not heard they understand.
> Isaiah 52:13—53:12

But this is the covenant that I will make with the house of Israel after those days, declares the LORD: I will put my law within them, and I will write it on their hearts. And I will be their God, and they shall be my people. Jeremiah 31:33

I will sprinkle clean water on you, and you shall be clean from all your uncleannesses, and from all your idols I will cleanse you. And I will give you a new heart, and a new spirit I will put within you. And I will remove the heart of stone from your flesh and give you a heart of flesh. And I will put my Spirit within you and cause you to walk in my statutes and be careful to obey my rules." Ezekiel 36:25–27

Behold, I send my messenger, and he will prepare the way before me. And the LORD whom you seek will suddenly come to his temple; and the messenger of the covenant in whom you delight, behold, he is coming, says the LORD of hosts. Malachi 3:1

These Old Testament prophecies secured the bride's price; the LORD God testified to his faithfulness in the midst of the Bride's sexualized immoralities.

2

Now, a selection of relevant Gospel assurances that further fortified the trustworthy Old Testament prophecies for the bride's price:

> An angel to Joseph, "[Mary] will bear a son, and you
> shall call his name Jesus, for he will save his people from
> their sins." Matthew 1:21

> Gabriel to Mary, "[Jesus] will be great and will be called
> the Son of the Most High. And the Lord God will give
> him the throne of his father David." Luke 1:32

> For even the Son of Man came not to be served but to
> serve, and to give his life as a ransom for many. Mark
> 10:45; Matthew 20:28

> And [Jesus] began to teach them that the Son of Man
> must suffer many things and be rejected by the elders
> and the chief priests and the scribes and be killed, and
> after three days rise again. Mark 8:31; Matthew 16:21;
> Luke 9:22

> The Son of Man is going to be delivered into the hands of
> men, and they will kill him. And when he is killed, after
> three days he will rise. Mark 9:31; Matthew 17:22–23;
> Luke 9:44

> See, we are going up to Jerusalem, and the Son of Man
> will be delivered over to the chief priests and the scribes,
> and they will condemn him to death and deliver him
> over to the Gentiles. And they will mock him and spit
> on him, and flog him and kill him. And after three days
> he will rise. Mark 10:33–34; Matthew 20:18–19; Luke
> 18:31–33

These holy and unblemished guarantees served to stabilize
the men and the women of the Church prior to the revelation of
the bride's price. She at the Crucifixion proved her extreme un-
worthiness of the Groom's love. He in the submission of the bride's
price verified his faithfulness.

Matthew, Mark, Luke, and John, Spirit-driven, eschatologically pressed respective Gospels to reveal the crucial bride's price, the Crucifixion.

> So they took Jesus, and he went out, bearing his own cross, to the place called The Place of a Skull, which in Aramaic is called Golgotha. There they crucified him, and with him two others, one on either side, and Jesus between them. Pilate also wrote an inscription and put it on the cross. It read, "Jesus of Nazareth, the King of the Jews." Many of the Jews read this inscription, for the place where Jesus was crucified was near the city, and it was written in Aramaic, in Latin, and in Greek. So the chief priests of the Jews said to Pilate, "Do not write 'The King of the Jews,' but rather, 'This man said, I am the King of the Jews.'" Pilate answered, "What I have written I have written." John 19:17–22; Matthew 27:32–54; Mark 15:21–37; Luke 23:26–49

The propitiating Crucifixion constituted the bride's price. Graciously, to affirm the forever betrothal/marriage, he gave his humanity to death to prove his eternal love for the Bride, the Church; in that dying and death, Jesus atoned for his Bride's sins and took into himself God's wrath—the wrath of God the Father for the Church's rejection of the Christ, Jesus' own wrath for the Church's rejection of his love, and the Spirit's wrath for rebuffing Jesus. With the Resurrection, Jesus had completed the work for which his Father had planned his humanity and into which the Spirit had poured eternal life. The victory of the Resurrection over sin and death eternally affirmed the Husband/Bride hope for the Consummation.

An Eighth Sum

With the Crucifixion Jesus gave his humanity to prove his eternal love for the Church. With the Resurrection, Jesus completed the work for which God the Father had commissioned his humanity, to which he had committed himself, and for which the Holy Spirit gave him life.

THE MARRIAGE OF CHRIST AND CHURCH

With the eye-raising Ascension, Jesus entered the heavens, from the seat of omnipotent authority to complete the evolution of the history of the world, central to which his loving preparation of the Bride for eschatological marriage feasting. Through the redemptive powers of the Gospel, Christ's Bride consciously and conscientiously submits to sanctification; with the bride's price in hand and in heart, she cleanses herself from all idolatrous and adulterous evils, in the great day to receive her Lord and Husband. Motivated now by his indefatigable love, all who make up the Bride, attentive men leading, dare not rest until cleansed of all fornicative passions.

1

For over the three days of the dying and death of Jesus' humanity, he with God the Father and God the Spirit created the Resurrection, the resurrection of his humanity. Knowing Jesus' resurrection empowers the Bride to cleanse herself in the blood of her Husband and the life-giving presence of the Holy Spirit. To believe the Resurrection, it is written:

> But on the first day of the week, at early dawn, [the women] went to the tomb, taking the spices they had prepared. And they found the stone rolled away from the tomb, but when they went in they did not find the body of the Lord Jesus. While they were perplexed about this, behold, two men stood by them in dazzling apparel. And as they were frightened and bowed their faces to the ground, the men said to them, "Why do you seek the living among the dead? He is not here, but has risen. Remember how he told you, while he was still in Galilee, that the Son of Man must be delivered into the hands of sinful men and be crucified and on the third day rise."

And they remembered his words, and returning from the tomb they told all this things to the eleven and to all the rest. Luke 24:1–9; Matthew 28:1–10; John 20:1–10

Men of Israel, hear these words: Jesus of Nazareth, a man attested to you by God with mighty works and wonders and signs that God did through him in your midst, as you yourselves know—this Jesus, delivered up according to the definite plan and foreknowledge of God, you crucified and killed by the hands of lawless men. God raised him up, loosing the pangs of death, because it was not possible for him to be held by it. Acts 2:22–24

Now I would remind you, brothers, of the gospel I preached to you, which you received, in which you stand, and by which you are being saved, if you hold fast to the word I preached to you—unless you believed in vain.

For I delivered to you as of first importance what I also received: that Christ died for our sins in accordance with the Scriptures, that he was buried, that he was raised on the third day in accordance with the Scriptures, and that he appeared to Cephas, then to the twelve. Then he appeared to more than five hundred brothers at one time, most whom are still alive, though some have fallen asleep. Then he appeared to James, then to all the apostles. Last of all, as to one untimely born, he appeared also to me. First Corinthians 15:1–8

And between the throne and the four living creatures and among the elders I saw a Lamb standing, as though it had been slain, with seven horns and with seven eyes, which are the seven spirits of God sent out into all the earth. Revelation 5:6

The Resurrection's historical actuality fascinates and inspires the Church every day to enter upon her new life, proof of her love for Christ Jesus.

2

On account of receiving the bride's price, the Bride's resurrection life permeates her people, making all willing and able to live out of the ransom the Christ revealed in the Crucifixion and Resurrection. She has been resurrected with the Lord and Savior who thus created the continuum in which redeemed men and women on ever new frontiers of holiness find each other for marriage. A selection of this riches:

> And there is salvation in no one else, for there is no other name under heaven given among men by which we must be saved. Acts 4:12

> But now the righteousness of God has been manifested apart from [the Oral Law], although the Law and the Prophets bear witness to it—the righteousness of God through faith in Jesus Christ for all who believe. For there is no distinction: for all have sinned and fall short of the glory of God, and are justified by his grace as a gift, through the redemption that is in Christ Jesus, whom God put forward as a propitiation by his blood, to be received by faith. This was to show God's righteousness, because in his divine forbearance he had passed over former sins. It was to show his righteousness at the present time, so that he might be just and the justifier of the one who has faith in Jesus. Romans 3:21-26

> For while we were still weak, at the right time Christ died for the ungodly. For one will scarcely die for a righteous person—though perhaps for a good person one would dare even to die—but God shows his love for us in that while we were still sinners, Christ died for us. Since, therefore, we have now been justified by his blood, much more shall we be saved by him from the wrath of God. For if while we were enemies we were reconciled to God by the death of his Son, much more, now that we are reconciled, shall we be saved by his life. More than that, we also rejoice in God through our Lord Jesus Christ,

through whom we have now received reconciliation.
Romans 5:6–1, 18–20

What then shall we say to [eternal marriage in Christ]?
If God is for us, who can be against us? He who did not
spare his own Son but gave him up for us all, how will he
not also with him graciously give us all things. Romans
8:31–32

Christ redeemed us from the curse of the [Oral Law] by
becoming a curse for us—for it is written, "Cursed be everyone who is hanged on a tree"—so that in Christ Jesus
the blessing of Abraham might come to the Gentiles, so
that we might receive the promised Spirit through faith.
Galatians 3:13–14

And you were dead in the trespasses and sins in which
you once walked, following the course of this world, following the prince of the power of the air, the spirit that is
now at work in the sons of disobedience—among whom
we all once lived in the passions of our flesh, carrying out
the desires of the body and the mind, and were by nature
children of wrath like the rest of mankind. But God, being rich in mercy, because of the great love with which
he loved us, even when we were dead in our trespasses,
made us live together with Christ—by grace you have
been saved—and raised us up with him and seated us
with him in the heavenly places in Christ Jesus, so that in
the coming ages he might show the immeasurable riches
of his grace in kindness toward us in Christ Jesus. For
by grace you have been saved through faith. And this is
not your own doing; it is the gift of God, not a result of
works, so that no one may boast. For we are his work-
manship, created in Christ Jesus for good works, which
God prepared beforehand, that we should walk in them.
Ephesians 2:1–10

Since then we have a great high priest who has passed
through the heavens, Jesus, the Son of God, let us hold
fast our confession. For we do not have a high priest
who is unable to sympathize with our weaknesses, but

one who in every respect has been tempted as we are, yet without sin. Let us then with confidence draw near to the throne of grace, that we may receive mercy and find grace to help in time of need. Hebrews 4:14–16

Beloved, I am writing you no new commandment, but an old commandment that you had from the beginning. The old commandment is the word that you have heard. At the same time, it is a new commandment that I am writing to you, which is true in him and in you, because the darkness is passing away and the true light is already shining. Whoever says he is in the light and hates his brother is still in the darkness. First John 2:7–9

Christ Jesus' resurrection, believed and lived, authorizes the Church every day to attend to her consummation hope.

3

In her multidimensional resurrection life, the intergenerational Bride enters through her dominating sanctification upon the liberalizing high road of submission, the men to Christ, the women to the men, no one left out, even . . .

. . . submitting to one another out of reverence for Christ.
Wives, submit to your own husbands, as to the Lord. For the husband is the head of the wife even as Christ is the head of the church, his body, and is himself its Savior. Now as the church submits to Christ, so also wives should submit in everything to their husbands.
Husbands, love your wives, as Christ loved the church and gave himself up for her, that he might sanctify her, having cleansed her by the washing of water with the word, so that he might present the church to himself in splendor, without spot or wrinkle or any such thing, that she might be holy and without blemish. In the same way husbands should love their wives as their own bodies. He who loves his wife loves himself. For no one ever hated his own flesh, but nourishes and cherishes it, just as Christ does the church, because we are members of his

body. "Therefore a man shall leave his father and mother and hold fast to his wife, and the two shall become one flesh."[11] This mystery is profound, and I am saying that it refers to Christ and the church. However, let each one of you love his wife as himself, and let the wife see that she respects her husband. Ephesians 5:21–33

Wives, submit to your husbands, as is fitting in the Lord. Husbands, love your wives, and do not be harsh with them. Colossian 3:18–19

As the Husband with serious energy prepares the marriage celebration gleaming on historical horizons, its joys incentivize the Bride to free herself from every idolatrous impurity.

Then [John] heard what seemed to be the voice of a great multitude, like the roar of many waters and like the sound of mighty peals of thunder, crying out,

"Hallelujah!
For the Lord our God,
the Almighty reigns.
Let us rejoice and exult and give him the glory,
for the marriage of the Lamb has come,
and his Bride has made herself ready;
it was granted her to clothe herself with fine linen,
bright and pure"—

for the fine linen is the righteous deeds of the saints.
And the angel said to me, "Write this: Blessed are those who are invited to the marriage supper of the Lamb." And he said to me, "These are the true words of God." Revelation 19:6–9

Then [John] saw a new heaven and a new earth, for the first heaven and the first earth had passed away, and the sea was no more. And I saw the holy city, new Jerusalem,

11. Genesis 2:24, "Therefore a man shall leave his father and his mother and hold fast to his wife, and they shall become one flesh."

coming down out of heaven from God, prepared as a bride adorned for her husband. Revelation 21:1–2

These catalytic passages daily reform the fundamental stabilizers of masculinity and femininity for human sexuality from Old Testament times throughout every present of the Church.

4

At the same time, the sovereign Lord Jesus granted breakthroughs to answer questions regarding remarriage, monogamy, devotions, childbearing, chastity, employment obligations; etc.

> . . . a married woman is bound by law to her husband while he lives, but if her husband dies she is released from the law of marriage. Accordingly, she will be called an adulteress if she lives with another man while her husband is alive. But if her husband dies, she is free from that law, and if she marries another man she is not an adulteress. Romans 7:2–3

> Now concerning the matters about which you wrote: "It is good for a man not to have sexual relations with a woman." But because of the temptation to sexual immorality, each man should have his own wife and each woman her own husband. The husband should give to his wife her conjugal rights, and likewise the wife to her husband. For the wife does not have authority over her own body, but the husband does. Likewise the husband does not have authority over his own body, but the wife does. Do not deprive one another, except perhaps by agreement for a limited time, that you may devote yourselves to prayer; but then come together again, so that Satan may not tempt you because of your lack of self-control. First Corinthians 7:1–5

> Now as a concession, not a command, I say this, I wish that all were as I myself am. But each has his own gift from God, one of one kind and one of another.
>
> To the unmarried and the widows I say that it is good to remain single as I am. But if they cannot exercise

self-control, they should marry. For it is better to marry than to burn with passion. First Corinthians 7:6–9

To the married I give this charge (not I, but the Lord): the wife should not separate from her husband (but if she does, she should remain unmarried or else be reconciled to her husband), and the husband should not divorce his wife. First Corinthians 7:10–11

As in all the churches of the saints, the women should keep silent in the churches. For they are not permitted to speak, but should be in submission, as the Law also says. If there is anything they desire to learn, let them ask their husbands at home. For it is shameful for a woman to speak in church.

Or was it from you that the word of God came? Or are you the only ones it has reached? If anyone thinks that he is a prophet, or spiritual, he should acknowledge that the things I am writing to you are a command of the Lord. If anyone does not recognize this, he is not recognized. First Corinthians 14:34–38

I desire then that in every place the men should pray, lifting holy hands without anger or quarreling, likewise also that women should adorn themselves in respectable apparel, with modesty and self-control, not with braided hair and gold or pearls or costly attire, but with what is proper for women who profess godliness—with good works. First Timothy 2:8–10

Let a woman learn quietly with all submissiveness. I do not permit a woman to teach or to exercise authority over a man; rather, she is to remain quiet. For Adam was formed first, then Eve; and Adam was not deceived, but the woman was deceived and became a transgressor. Yet she will be saved through childbearing—if they continue in faith and love and holiness, with self-control. First Timothy 2:11–15

Let marriage be held in honor among all, and let the marriage bed be undefiled, for God will judge the sexually immoral and adulterous. Hebrews 13:4

. . . wives, be subject to your own husbands, so that even if some do not obey the word, they may be won without a word by the conduct of their wives, when they see your respectful and pure conduct. Do not let your adorning be external—the braiding of hair and the putting on of gold jewelry, or the clothing you wear—but let your adorning be the hidden person of the heart with the imperishable beauty of a gentle and quiet spirit, which in God's sight is very precious. For this is how the holy women who hoped in God used to adorn themselves, by submitting to their own husbands, as Sarah obeyed Abraham, calling him lord.[12] And you are her children, if you do good and do not fear anything that is frightening.[13] First Peter 3:1–6

. . . husbands, live with your wives in an understanding way, showing honor to the woman as the weaker vessel,[14] since they are heirs with you of the grace of life, so that your prayers may not be hindered. First Peter 3:7

A Ninth Sum

These biblical directives sanitize the male/female stabilizers for married living, husbands for wives, wives for husbands, specifically in one-flesh sexuality. With love, respect, and trust, husbands rather than "rape" respective wives, using them for physical satisfaction, ensure the wives too, simultaneously, receive orgiastic

12. Genesis 18:12, "So Sarah laughed to herself, saying, 'After I am worn out, and my lord is old, shall I have pleasure?'"

13. Paganizing public opinion about Christianity may be frightening, twisting men of faith into masochists and forcing women of faith in feminists. They who perceive strength as weakness and wisdom as folly stumble into the end, confronted by a closed door, incapacitated for an eleventh-hour conversion.

14. The "weaker vessel" refers to Eve's status as Adam's helper. Genesis 2:18.

consummation, in this manner confirming the husband/wife union. And wives, instead of laying back and suffering husbands to use their bodies for self-gratification or find sex a way to manipulate husbands, which is a form of prostitution, insist on synchronized climaxing, together rejoicing in this marital bonding.

Sexual intercourse, a multivalent communication, may express joys of marriage, hopes for children, even a longing for the final consummation of the timeless Christ/Church bond. In this animated and communicative way, husbands long for wives and wives for husbands, even as Eve had for Adam.

THE TESTING OF HUMAN SEXUALITY

Acknowledging the Church as the Bride, the men leading in submission to the Word and the women following, whatever the cultural winds, every congregation remembers the carnal strictures of the Old Testament and incorporates these in her living deference to the New Testament Scriptures. At the same time, the Bride's preparing for the consummation exposes the New Testament parameters of holiness; in that process, she bans pretentions at freedom that men may be women and women men. Breaking with the commandments regarding human sexuality compels concentration on anomaly and abnormality. Sexual vagaries bring on slavery to human identity confused by constantly altering desires and fashions. In leading up to the wedding, the Bride hears her Lord, the Bridegroom of terrifying splendor, and finds him cleansing her of spots or wrinkles or any such things. He wills her holy and righteous.

In the New Testament submission language faithfully translated the *middle* form of *apotasso*, Ephesians 5:21–24; Colossians 3:18; 1 Peter 3:1–6. "Be subject to" and "submission" picked up Genesis 2:18 as well as Genesis 3:16 for the New Testament Church and applied to all women in Christ. Yearnings for undue liberation through illicit interpretations of freedom, which Hellenistic cultural influences stimulated, made Paul and Peter reemphasize "help meet for" in the early Church. Thus, the apostles startled women in Christ's Church out of Hellenistic conventions and expectations. Since *apotasso* carried meanings of subordination and surrender, the Lord Jesus called the women of the Church to stop rebelling, as Eve had, to live as active members of the covenant communion by subjecting themselves to respective husbands. At the same time the Lord of the Church led covenant men to carry congenital accountability for wives and daughters, mothers and sisters. He upended abuse of and misuse over them, or take advantage of them, according to misshapen authoritarian conventions.

1

In each of the following selections, the Bridegroom summons the men and the women of the Bride to submission, sanctification; these interconnected prohibitions and injunctions spell out tensions inherent in human sexuality, either the way of the Bridegroom or the ways of men and of women at satisfying the sexual urges of the flesh. He wills no more abuse of human bodies through pagan Western values and stimulants. He wills his astounding truth in stabilizing masculinity and femininity, not any and every unregulated consensus for carnality. Consider:

> [On account of swelling idolatry] God gave them up in the lusts of their hearts to impurity, to the dishonoring of their bodies among themselves, because they exchanged the truth about God for a lie and worshiped and served the creature rather than the Creator, who is blessed forever! Amen.
>
> For this reason God gave them up to dishonorable passions. For their women exchanged natural relations for those that are contrary to nature; and the men likewise gave up natural relations with women and were consumed with passion for one another, men committing shameful acts with men and receiving in themselves the due penalty for their error.[15] Romans 1:24–27

---

15. First Corinthians 6:18: "Every other sin a person commits is outside the body, but the sexual immoral person sins against his own body."

. . . since they did not see fit to acknowledge God, God gave them up to a debased mind to do what ought not to be done. They were filled with all manner of unrighteousness, evil, covetousness, malice. They are full of envy, murder, strife, deceit, maliciousness. They are gossips, slanderers, haters of God, insolent, haughty, boastful, inventors of evil, disobedient to parents, foolish, faithless, heartless, ruthless. Though they know God's decree that those who practice such things deserve to die, they not only do them but give approval to those who practice them. Romans 1:28–32

. . . you know the time, that the hour has come for you to wake from sleep. For salvation is nearer to us now than when we first believed. The night is far gone; the day is at hand. So then let us cast off the works of darkness and put on the armor of light. Let us walk properly as in the daytime, not in orgies and drunkenness, not in sexual immorality and sensuality, not in quarreling and jealousy. But put on the Lord Jesus Christ, and make no provision for the flesh, to gratify its desires. Romans 13:11–14

"All things are lawful for me," but not all things are helpful. "All things are lawful for me," but I will not be enslaved by anything. "Food is meant for the stomach and the stomach for food"—and God will destroy both one and the other. The body is not meant for sexual immorality, but for the Lord, and the Lord for the body. And God raised the Lord and will also raise us up by his power. Do you not know that your bodies are members of Christ? Shall I then take the members of Christ and make them members of a prostitute? Never! Or do you not know that he who is joined to a prostitute becomes one body with her? For, as it is written, "The two will become one flesh."[16] But he who is joined to the Lord becomes one spirit with him. Flee from sexual immorality. Every other sin a person commits is outside the body, but the sexually immoral person sins against his own body. Or do you not know that your body is a temple of the Holy Spirit

16. Genesis 2:24, "Therefore a man shall leave his father and his mother and hold fast to his wife, and they shall become one flesh."

within you, whom you have from God? You are not your own, for you were bought with a price. So glorify God in your body. First Corinthians 6:12–20

Now the works of the flesh are evident: sexual immorality, impurity, sensuality, idolatry, sorcery, enmity, strife, jealousy, fits of anger, rivalries, dissensions, divisions, envy, drunkenness, orgies, and things like these. I warn you, as I warned you before, that those who do such things will not inherit the kingdom of God. Galatians 5:19–22

Now this I say and testify in the Lord, that you must no longer walk as the Gentiles do, in the futility of their minds. They are darkened in their understanding, alienated from the life of God because of the ignorance that is in them, due to their hardness of heart. They have become callous and have given themselves up to sensuality, greedy to practice every kind of impurity. But that is not the way you learned Christ!—assuming that you have heard about him and were taught in him, as the truth is in Jesus, to put off your old self, which belongs to your former manner of life and is corrupt through deceitful desires, and to be renewed in the spirit of your minds, and to put on the new self, created after the likeness of God in true righteousness and holiness. Ephesians 4:17–24

Look out for the dogs, look out for the evildoers, look out for those who mutilate the flesh. Philippians 3:2

Put to death, therefore what is earthly in you, sexual immorality, impurity, passion, evil desire, and covetousness, which is idolatry. On account of these the wrath of God is coming. In these you too once walked, when you were living in them. But now you must put them all away: anger, wrath, malice, slander, and obscene talk from your mouth. Do not lie to one another, seeing that you have put off the old self with its practices, and have put on the new self, which is being renewed in knowledge after the image of its creator. Here there is not Greek and Jew, circumcised and uncircumcised, barbarian, Scythian, slave, free, but Christ is all, and in all.

Put on then, as God's chosen ones, holy and beloved, compassionate hearts, kindness, humility, meekness, and patience, bearing with one another and, if one has a complaint against another, forgiving each other; as the Lord has forgiven you, so you also must forgive. And above all these put on love, which binds everything together in perfect harmony. And let the peace of Christ rule in your hearts, to which indeed you were called in one body. And be thankful. Let the word of Christ dwell in you richly, teaching and admonishing one another in all wisdom, singing psalms and hymns and spiritual songs, with thankfulness in your hearts to God. And whatever you do, in word and deed, do everything in the name of the Lord Jesus, giving thanks to God the Father through him. Colossians 3:5–17

For this is the will of God, your sanctification: that you abstain from sexual immorality; that each one of you know how to control his own body in holiness and honor, not in the passion of lust like the Gentiles who do not know God; that no one transgress and wrong his brother in this matter, because the Lord is an avenger in all these things, as we told you beforehand and solemnly warned you. For God has not called us for impurity, but in holiness. First Thessalonians 4:3–7

Now the Spirit expressly says that in later times some will depart from the faith by devoting themselves to deceitful spirits and teachings of demons, through the insincerity of liars whose consciences are seared, who forbid marriage and require abstinence from foods that God created to be received with thanksgiving by those who believe and know the truth. First Timothy 4:1–3

But understand this, that in the last days there will come times of difficulty. For people will be lovers of self, lovers of money, proud, arrogant, abusive, disobedient to their parents, ungrateful, unholy, heartless, unappeasable, slanderous, without self-control, brutal, not loving good, treacherous, reckless, swollen with conceit, lovers of pleasure rather than lovers of God, having the appearance of godliness, but denying its power. Second Timothy 3:1–5

In your struggle against sin you have not yet resisted to the point of shedding your blood. Hebrews 12:4

What causes quarrels and what causes fights among you? Is it not this, that your passions are at war within you? You desire and do not have, so you murder. You covet and cannot obtain, so you fight and quarrel. You do not have, because you do not ask. You ask and do not receive, because you ask wrongly, to spend it on your passions. You adulterous people! James 4:1–4a

. . . husbands, live with your wives in an understanding way, showing honor to the woman as the weaker vessel, since they are heirs with you of the grace of life, so that your prayers may not be hindered. First Peter 3:7

Bold and willful, they do not tremble as they blaspheme the glorious ones, whereas angels, though greater in might and power, do not pronounce a blasphemous judgment against them before the Lord. But these, like irrational animals, creatures of instinct, born to be caught and destroyed, blaspheming about matters of which they are ignorant, will also be destroyed in their destruction, suffering wrong as the wage for their wrongdoings. They count it pleasure to revel in the daytime. They are blots and blemishes, reveling in their deceptions, while they feast with you. They have eyes full of adultery, insatiable for sin. Second Peter 2:10b–14b

Everyone who believes that Jesus is the Christ has been born of God, and everyone who loves the Father loves whoever has been born of him. By this we know that we love the children of God, when we love God and obey his commandments. For this is the love of God,[17] that

17. The now hard, infertile Western soil resists love's complex and powerful force.

we keep his commandments. And his commandments are not burdensome. For everyone who has been born of God overcomes the world. And this is the victory that has overcome the world—our faith. Who is it that overcomes the world, except the one who believes that Jesus is the Son of God. First John 5:1–5

Yet in like manner these people also, relying on their dreams, defile the flesh, reject authority, and blaspheme the glorious ones. But when the archangel Michael, contending with the devil, was disputing about the body of Moses, he did not presume to pronounce a blasphemous judgment, but said, "The Lord rebuke you." But these people blaspheme all that they do not understand, and they are destroyed by all that they, like unreasoning animals, understand instinctively. Woe to them! For they walked in the way of Cain and abandoned themselves for the sake of gain to Balaam's error and perished in Korah's rebellion. These are hidden reefs at your love feasts, as they feast with you without fear, shepherds feeding themselves; waterless clouds, swept along by winds; fruitless trees in late autumn twice dead, uprooted; wild waves of the sea, casting up the foam of their own shame; wandering stars, for whom the gloom of utter darkness has been reserved forever. Jude 8–13

I know your works, your love and faith and service and patient endurance, and that your latter works exceed the first. But I have this against you, that you tolerate that woman Jezebel, who calls herself a prophetess and is teaching and seducing my servants to practice sexual immorality and to eat food sacrificed to idols. I gave her time to repent, but she refuses to repent of her sexual immorality. Behold, I will throw her onto a sickbed, and those who commit adultery with her I will throw into great tribulation, unless they repent of her works, and I will strike her children dead. Revelation 2:19–23a

Sexual temptations subvert masculinity into cynical masochism and femininity into sarcastic feminism to do whatever satisfies carnal lusting in violation of human connubiality —physically, emotionally, mentally, and spiritually—making all who surrender to this vulnerability stand naked and unprotected before the Judge of all the earth, Christ Jesus. Until *the* day of the Lord, the testing goes on.

2

These direct proscriptions and prohibitions, contextualized, represent the Bridegroom's headship commandments to the Bride that, she through sanctification, strip off every sexual immorality (along with all the others). When masculinity and femininity have free play, the Groom grounds the Bride in the eternality of the eschatological consummation.

To be sure, in the generational struggles for gender superiority to identify as well as differentiate masculinity and femininity, physicalities often prevail to disguise masochism and feminism. When females optimize body language with hair styles, clothing fashions, and ornamental charms, they camouflage feminism, thereby denying that femininity is a matter of the heart, to know oneself as a woman in Christ. Counterpointing, when males optimize body language with grooming flairs, modish clothing, and chauvinistic bravado, they conceal masochism, crowding out the reality that masculinity is a matter of the heart, to know oneself as a man in Christ. Since the beginning of the Recreation, directly after Adam's Fall, Adam and Eve initiated the deep things of manhood and womanhood at the center of which the love of God and the love of spouses.

3

The contemporary Church, swaying under weights of Western values and seduced by allures of fornicative pleasures, suffers the testing of human sexuality, the idolatrous as well as therewith the carnal. Temptations to submit to these erotic urges and conform to

Westernized sexualized pleasures tempt congregations and members to revive enslaving life choices totally at odds with the Word of God. Each misallocation of human sexuality abuses the Bride and angers the Bridegroom.

. . . . .

Eighteenth-century industrialization and twentieth-century technolization/digitalization required a modernized idolatry to legitimate carelessness in matters of sexual intimacies. In the Western heart, industrial magnates and digitalized tycoons, to control the general public, invented and handled the widespread adoption of demonic images to depersonalize marriage centered strengths; in the aggregation of authority and economic dominance, these handlers invented the masochist Man and his consort, the feminist Woman. To adulate these invisible gods, magnates and tycoons hired advertisers to advertise the people-pleasing fallacies of the present and synthesize contagious fornicative forces; these advocates not only anticipate, they also scorch consciences to eliminate gatherings of guilt. Alongside the handlers and prophets, with conniving psychologists/psychiatrists as priests smoothen out as well as cover up damages caused by sexual dysfunction; these lackeys mitigate pains of deep sinning and sublimate carnal brokenness. Now fully enthroned in the twenty-first century's culture, the Man and the Woman entice true believers to ignore with impunity the consequences of carnality in order to excite more good feelings, all deaf to the reechoing censure—"Vanity, all is vanity."

The two dominant spirits of the West, for individualizing and depersonalizing human sexuality, position deceptive road signs that counter bipolar Adam-and-Eve marriages. Handlers and marketers of the Man and the Woman persuade Western citizenry to self-fulfillment in carnal pleasures, the inconvenience of children, and a contrary version of the good life. The Man and the Woman's marketers mock life-long marital obligations and family commitments; instead, they electrify passions for alternate forms of human sexuality, inciting fornicative cravings in the general populace.

This retrograde paganizing of human sexuality demands social acceptance for the vagaries of killing the unborn, indiscriminate contraception, premarital sex, extra-marital intimacies, (gray) divorce, pedophilia, pederasty, prostitution (aka sex work), pornography, homosexuality/homosexualism, lesbianism, bigamy, polygamy/polyamory, cohabitation, eroticism, reproductive freedom, gender identity, childless marriages, masturbation, voyeurism; etc. These escapes into permissiveness identify the low roads of Western civilization. Fearlessly, the worshipers of the Man and the Woman despise the Husband of the Church; they will lead his Bride into sexualized disasters for acceptance in public opinions, community standards, and Western values in order to obfuscate the Scriptures. These overpowering opinions, standards, and values free citizens for careers, travels, and creaturely comforts.

In the realm of the Man and the Woman, children hamper careering, social mobility, and indulgence in luxury. This anti-procreativity, part of a wider trending, insists on fewer children or the avoidance of parenthood altogether, which places Christian men and women before as well as in a spiritual intermingling that curtails childbirth in the Church and in the Kingdom. Is not this also integral to the Serpent's warfare against the omnipotently regnant Christ? This intermingling in Western values also has the men abhor post-partum bellies. Now, in the continuation of migration to the cities, with the intensification of women's education, and through the appeals to own Western creature comforts, the inflationary costs of raising children alarms women to limit the number of children they will bear.

Nevertheless, the longsuffering Bridegroom summons the (men of the) Bride to headship and to reformation, to own the actualities of married life, lest the prerogatives of marriage suffer and the nuptial directives fall as rubbish by the wayside.

. . . . .

As the Lord Jesus develops the paganizing West, amidst complexities of equality and the complications of complementarity, he drops fertility rates, statistically, to prove the reprobation of unbelievers. At the-time, he wills more members in the Church and citizens for the Kingdom to fill out the finite 144,000 symbolized in *The Apocalypse*, the last Bible book. Throughout the centuries of the New Testament dispensation, he faithfully completes the number of the elect, which ingathering of the Church excites birthing sons and daughters, each a gift. Therefore, every husband/wife union before wedlock and throughout the years of fertility owns raising children to glorify the Lord Jesus as a primary family care.

A Tenth Sum

Nuptial preparation requires the Church in the West 1) to fight off novel gods, 2) to assume the divine commandments, and 3) to gain an eschatological arc in living, free from enslavements. In other words, the Bride, listening to her Husband, fights the pretentious masochist and feminist masters of the universe in which broken men make the rules and jealous women fight men.

Even in aging, as debilitating sicknesses and physical deteriorations settle sexual passions, for all on the high road, the male/female bond of sexuality may be resolved with simple sex, quietly holding hands and remembering the intimacies of the past.

THE LASTING SUM

SIMPLY, BY *CATALOGUING* MARITAL commitments and carnal prohibitions, the Christ confronts his Bride most directly with lasting obligations. No sanctifying? No participation in the wedding feast! All outside the Faith mock the Husband. All on the verge of the Faith nod agreeably, only to compromise and continue in carnal sinning. All of the Faith seek the cleansing of the Bride.

> Therefore lift your drooping hands and strengthen your weak knees, and make straight paths for your feet, so that what is lame may not be put out of joint but rather be

healed.[18] Strive for peace with everyone, and for the holiness without which no one will see the Lord. See to it that no one fails to obtain the grace of God; that no 'root of bitterness' springs up and causes trouble, and by it many become defiled; that no one is sexually immoral or unholy like Esau, who sold his birthright for a single meal. For you know that afterwards, when he desired to inherit the blessing, he was rejected, for he found no chance to repent, though he sought it with tears. Hebrews 12:12–17

Without actual cleansing away sexualized sinning, hopes for the consummation may linger on the fringes, and eventually, at critical moments, come to nothing.

---

18. Isaiah 35:3, "Strengthen the weak hands, and make firm the feeble knees."

www.ingramcontent.com/pod-product-compliance
Lightning Source LLC
Chambersburg PA
CBHW052137090426

42741CB00009B/2114